Giovanni Pietro Orefice

The secrets of the hidden canons in J.S. Bach's masterpieces

Die Geheimnisse der verborgenen Kanons von J.S. Bach

I segreti dei canoni nascosti nei capolavori di J.S. Bach

Les secrets des canons cachés de J.S. Bach

Büchlein für Johann Sebastian

First Edition – Prima Edizione

Giovanni Pietro Orefice

The secrets of the hidden canons in J.S. Bach's masterpieces

Die Geheimnisse der verborgenen Kanons von J.S. Bach

I segreti dei canoni nascosti nei capolavori di J.S. Bach

Les secrets des canons cachés de J.S. Bach

Büchlein für Johann Sebastian

First Edition – Prima Edizione

ISBN | 979-12-21485-40-0

Cover Image: *COVER_BachsCanonsBook*
by Giovanni Pietro Orefice copyright: CC by-nc-nd 4.0
https://creativecommons.org/licenses/by-nc-nd/4.0/
https://www.patamu.com/certificate/196123-2d1
derived from
Bach By Elias Gottlob Haussmann – httpwww.jsbach.netbasselementsbach-hausmann.jpg , Public Domain,
httpscommons.wikimedia.orgwindex.phpcurid=1270015
contact: giovanni.pietro.orefice@gmail.com https://metamusica.altervista.org/

Many thanks to, *mille grazie a***, herzlichen Dank zu,** *un grand Merci à*
Catherine Ambroise et François Regairaz pour la révision en français.
Catherine Ambroise, Martin Polster, Frank Nöltner für die Sanierung.

INDEX

The secrets of the hidden canons in J.S. Bach's masterpieces

Büchlein für Johann Sebastian

Introduction

When listening the music of the great composer J.S. Bach, everyone can experience a deep resonance of his melodies in the soul. Moreover, when listening the organ masterpieces of J.S. Bach in a reverberant church a distinctive clearness may impress you when comparing it to masterpieces of other musicians. In this book I'll try to get more insight and to explain both of these experiences, on the basis of the recent research that I performed to unveil the hidden canons in many famous works of J.S. Bach and that I will present in detail.

This book is very short and, I hope, written in an easy understandable way compared to more technical specialistic musicology works. The aim is to inspire musicians and musicologists, offering many starting points for more orthodox research works. The book will be a guide for all of the fans of Bach's music, who will discover in the linked audio samples the beauty of the multiple canons, and will better understand the indescribable sensation and effect that they are experiencing when listening J.S. Bach's works.

In despite of any expectation, three centuries after its composition the work of J.S. Bach still reserves a lot of surprises and hidden treasures. The first part of this booklet presents the wide musicology research I developed on a paramount reference in the history of music such as J.S. Bach, to unveil the immanent multiple canon structure in his work, unnoticed until now. As cello player, I discovered this hidden structure starting from the solo Cello Suites, then going on with the Partitas and Sonatas for solo Violin, the unachieved Suite for solo Flute, the French and

English Suites for Piano, with some additional pieces to complete the missed movements and I ended exploring some concertos for orchestra and soloists. Exposing this work, I will evidence unexpected rhythmical effects and unachieved/missed parts in some pieces, proposing some ways of completing it and providing some answers to old disputes and attribution problems. I further will explain the complexity of composing multiple canons and provide a comparison with some famous pieces of other composers of Bach's time to let emerge a new insight on his outstanding capabilities and talents.

In the second part of the book, I'll present an innovative thesis, based on my competences and studies in the field of Acoustics and Psycho-Acoustics, coupled to my music performer's experiences and reflections. This peculiar approach provides an explanation of the practical and tactical reasons of J.S. Bach to pervasively hide multiple canons in his melody lines, as presented in the first part. This theory will permit to highlight how Bach was facing and solving, as improviser and composer, some typical performer's problems, getting an immediate advantage in his improvisation competitions. The thesis further holds up that Bach was instinctively understanding some psycho-acoustics effects and decided to adopt this "secret ingredient" to compose masterpieces and get a worldwide success.

If you are not interested in technical details of the canon's structures and about the discovery process of the hidden canons, but you want to know why J.S. Bach was hiding it, just jump to the second part of this short book, at chapter 5, but reading another ten pages won't kill you!

PART I CANONS, not CANNONS

1 Visible canons and hidden, immanent canons

To read about the hidden canons discovery jump to chapter 2.

The matter of the following chapter is to distinguish between the canons that are explicitly visible in Bach's compositions and the hidden ones that will be treated in the second chapter.

Some words about the usual understanding of the Canons of J.S. Bach

The most famous and developed canons of J.S. Bach are the 10 explicitly written in the Musical Offering BWV 1079 for the Prussia king, see [1], very appreciated by Anton von Webern who developed the *Ricercare* in 1935. Bach also wrote the canonical variations on "Von Himmel hoch" (for organ) BWV 769 as a presentation piece for the Mizler Society in Leipzig, of which he became a member in 1747. These two works show how important the canonical form was for him, and how high he was praising his own ability to handle with it, to consider it as a presentation card and even a valuable gift for a king. A canon can even be found in Anna Magdalena's Büchlein (Canon, BWV Anh.120), elected in this way as highest love gift.

Beside the previous musical pieces his short canons BWV 1072-86 were known and mostly classified as pedagogic staff for his pupils and children, or exercises/occasional small piece (BWV 1073), or, on the contrary, sanctified (canon triplex BWV 1076) [9]. See for instance the first canon in Fig.1.

Figure 1: One can observe there that the melody line is oscillating, like a wave, a sinus function and that there are four voices fitting within the bars lines and four voices (the intermediate ones) overlapping it and creating a more complex rhythmical effect. The same element is repeated infinitely. A ninth voice would of course be identical with the first one.

In the Kunst der Fugue BWV 1080 as well Bach was clearly showing 4 voices canons and complex structures ("canon alla duodecima in contrapunto alla quinta; due canoni per augmentationem in contrario motu") and these pieces are not considered mere exercises.

The very late discovery of the 14 Canons BWV 1087, a single page (see Fig.2) found in 1974 at the end of Bach's personal copy of the Goldberg Variations, showed how refined and complex the canon structure and design could be in his mind, adding vertical and horizontal symmetries and exploring also the time augmentations and diminutions, additionally to the usual time shift of the canons. It is a true canons guide, that was largely discussed, explained and illustrated, see for instance [2], [3], [4], [5].

Figure 2: BWV 1087 Holograph manuscript, n.d.(ca.1741-46)
https://imslp.org/wiki/File:PMLP326356-N55005962_(BWV_1087).pdf

Furthermore the 13th canon corresponds to the one illustrated in the Portrait of J.S. Bach by Elias Gottlob Haussmann (1746), so this precious single page document was containing what he thought to be the most important legacy of his life!

As "consequence" or side-effect of this discovery some "studies" like [6a], [7], [8] appeared about the mathematical transformation functions that describe the canons building processes: however, these works can just be used to implement new tools for modern composer's software and don't provide any relevant musical knowledge.

In 1867 Helfer, Friedrich August with his *Canon für 2 Clav. u. Pedal BACH über Bach,* In: Album für die Orgel zu J. G.Töpfer's goldner Amts-Jubelfeier am 4. Juni 1867. - Weimar: T. F. A. Kühn, 1867, S. 54-55, was exploring a hidden canon in a piece for organ.

However, the capability of J.S. Bach to compose multiple canons in major works was just tasted in the 10th piece of the Musical Offer BWV 1079 (*Canon a 4 quaerendo invenietis*) and never was properly discovered and appreciated during his life: the bellicose Prussian king was not impressed during his visit, maybe he was told that a Canon expert was coming and misunderstanding it he was expecting to meet an expert of Cannons for his wars!

More seriously, J.S. Bach's theoretical legacy left in his above cited lessons, guides and small books for his beloved children & wife seemed not to have been fully applied in major pieces and his consideration of the canons as his highest form of creation couldn't be fully understood …

Till now I was just speaking about the explicit canons visible in different pieces, more or less easy to be heard and recognized (surely nowadays, thanks to the pedagogic videos of [10]) and completely known by the musicology and by many musicians to. The matter of this book is on the contrary the unknown immanent canons that are hidden in many works, that remained secret and that I'm unveiling here after three centuries of hardly understandable and unforgivable inattentions.

2 Unveiling Bach's hidden canons: a passionate journey

2.1 *Some words about the Suites of J.S. Bach*

The Suite of dances is a musical form that reflects a double French influence on J.S. Bach. The most evident influence is his (and more generally spoken the small German courts') fascination for the great Court of France of the sunny Louis XIV, with its dances that fully belong to the conventional representation of the King's domination over the Nobles and over the court's Ladies as well. Another more subtle influence was the philosophical one, that starting from Descartes (and travelling through a more complex Spinoza) arrived to Leibniz, who was surely dominating the German way of thinking and believing at Bach's time: the necessity of the harmony, the sense of a structured universe, full of order and beauty, reflecting the perfection of its divine creator. In Bach's country the order was appreciated and driven by the austere guide of the church of Luther and Calvin (especially austere after the terrible time of the Anabaptists extermination in the region of Bach), opposed to the diverse, incoherent, lax, but more fantasy and improvisation-full word of the catholic church, with its special effects of the virtuosi concertos (that were fascinating Bach and surely inspiring him, both for composing and improvising).

The baroque Suite of dances is starting by an overture, followed by an alternation of dances of different speeds, requiring more or less physical effort, typically the Allemande, Courante, Sarabande and Gigue. After the 17th-century further dances were integrated between the previous ones, like the Minuets, Bourrées, Gavottes, Passepieds, Rigaudons... For the Cello Suites a famous French predecessor was Marin Marais (1656-1728) with his *Pièces de viole*, that were surely influencing Bach's work: the first book (1686) of these Pièces was in fact a very complete Suite (Prelude – Fantaisie – Allemande – Double – Courante – Double – Sarabande – Gigue – Double) and explains Bach's use of the names "Double" and "Phantasie" for his compositions. *The Suitte d'un Goût Étranger* of Marin Marais was impressively concatenating 33 dances!

Bach always added a couple of such "dances galantes" in the Cello Suites, or doubled some other piece like the Courante, or inserted a couple of twin pieces called "Doubles", or inserted foreign dances like the Siciliana, or mixed several pieces just indicating each speed/character, as in the Violin Partitas and Sonatas, with the Prestos, Adagios, Allegros and so on.

J.S. Bach proposed his solo instrument Suites as a genial way to entertain a small court, with a modest (cheap), single musician for a very complete dancing time, comparable to the ideal French court's one, including the Prelude as, both, musically interesting piece, possibly adding to it the complexity of a Fugue, and dances-preparation piece, for an assembly of speaking people, equivalent to a modern "piano bar" time. At the same time his precious works transmits a clear sense of being strongly structured and the melodies go in deep in the listener soul, creating a sense of discovering a true translation into sounds of the beauty of the universe. There are a lot of musicology discussions about the style of many dances, being more Italian than French, however the most important there is the global intent of these unique works. Also, the so-called English Suites were composed and offered in the hope to be played at the English court, but still with the intent to recreate the French court's ambiance and splendour.

We also may distinguish between the Suites for Harpsichord, that is a polyphonic instrument, normally used as "standalone" device, pieces that were mostly composed before the Köthen period, and those for solo Cello/Violin/Flute. The latter were challenging to be composed, because these pieces had to animate a musical dancing session with one melodic instrument only, which often happened for folk music in some square, or tavern, or ship, but risked not being enough for a Royal Court. In fact, these solo Cello/Violin/Flute Suites could have thought as ideal "travelling set" for the often-moving Prince Leopold of Köthen, who could extremely reduce the travel expenses for his accompanying musicians.

Last remark: the meditative wandering character of many pieces of the Cello and of the Violin Suites, that all of us have in mind, is actually our heritage of the late romantic interpretations of the past century considering the Suites as pure music (or mere instrumental exercises!). In the last decades many interpreters showed that the dances of the Cello Suites can fully be played as dances, with their original and dominant rhythmical character. The Suites for Harpsichord didn't endure such a strong romantic misreading.

2.2   Unveiling the secrets of the second Cello Suite

2.2.1   The Prelude of the second Suite

While playing the Suites "a Cello Solo senza basso" in a woody room (a small octagonal chapel in the French mountains, quite reverberant and with echoes) in 1984 I remarked a strange sound effect: I had the impression to accompanying myself, to enhance the marvellous pieces of J.S. Bach. This impressed me a lot and I promised to myself to further investigate this phenomenon. In 1991's summer playing the Prelude of the 2nd Cello Suite, I listened attentively the melody and deeper analysed it finding that the entire piece worked as a Canon.

I (badly) developed the final chords of the Prelude, to be compliant with the canon till the send of the piece and I printed it as shown in Figure 3, for two Cellos, and for Violin and Cello as well. When testing it with a friend some years later he remarked that some parts were not working well, so I promised to myself again to have a better look on it. In 2019 I finally found the occasion to analyse the problematic parts and to find a solution changing many notes using a basic software on a PC. It took some time, because these sections were really not compatible with a canon and the melody had to be completely transformed. By the way the first questions came in my mind: why Bach didn't do it correctly like for the rest of the piece? I couldn't find an answer to this question, but I had a look on the score and I

Figure 3: 2nd Cello Suite, 2 voices canon

had an intuition: there was still place for adding a third voice, I tried it immediately and I discovered that the Prelude was working indeed as 3 voices canon.

I will explain later why it was now a much bigger problem for me finding a proper solution for the missed, not compliant sections. It took many days and the solution never was satisfying me: the proposed music lines were far away to be comparable with Bach's (?) splendid original work for solo Cello, and some corrections on single notes in the rest of the piece were necessary as well to be compliant with a 3 voices canon. Even more recently, in 2023, I tried to find better solutions (and I succeeded at least for the chords development), but the missed sections are still resisting.

My explanation for the fact that the sections didn't work as canons in the original piece (that was identical in both the Anna Magdalena's and the Kellner's editions) was that J.S. Bach had composed it just before his first wife's sudden death, letting a "hole" corresponding to the problematic sections "to be finished after" and letting the final chords to be developed as well. Probably he never found the mood to complete it, and this painful piece was completed by the talented and elegant Anna Magdalena Wilcke. Another version is that nobody understood why he was wasting so many time for completing a simple piece for Cello alone, so he badly did it in hurry to close the Suites (and to sell it); but I don't believe this, because the Suites were first given to his pupil Kellner and published much later. Maybe he had to let use it by Kellner or by another Cellist at some occasion (a dancing session), in any case the original scope of providing a masterpiece as gift for the prince Leopold, who was playing the Viola da Gamba, had failed, because the prince was not a great player and the Suites were not easy to be played, so there was no hurry for finishing it.

2.2.2 The undeveloped final chords

After this discovery, the very old dispute matter between Cellists, about *developing or not developing the final chords* of the Prelude of the 2nd Suite, tends to find a solution: because of the short time shift, one could accept a inelegant "shorter chords solution", like that of Fig. 5, to avoid overlapping them when played in the original length, but in my mind the chords <u>must</u> be developed (otherwise the triple canon doesn't work), it must be done respecting the hidden triple canon structure. I'm proposing hereafter a solution in Fig. 6.

Figure 4: chords in the original scores

Figure 5: chords in the acceptable form for a 3 voices canon

Figure 6: the 3 voices canon final chords development

2.3   *Unveiling the rest of the second solo Cello Suite*

So long I thought that this discovery of a beautiful 3 voices canon in such a long and complex piece as the Prelude was a remarkable unicum in the music history, but just to try it, I extended the analysis to the following dances of the 2nd Suite, i.e., the Allemande, the Courante, the Sarabande, the two Menuets and the Gigue. I had to copy note by note all of the score, it was an intensive work at the end of 2021; thanks to this I found out that every dance was actually written to be compliant with a 3 voices canon; there were no other major problems like those encountered in the Prelude: excepted for a few notes, no correction was needed. This was even a greater surprise than for the Prelude, because each time one starts to analyse a piece and adds the other voices, one cannot imagine and hear in advance the canon, especially working on music masterpieces one is playing and hearing since years and years: I was sitting on a treasure box without having noticed it!

I shared the resulting scores on a couple of public websites (IMSLP and AIMA music) and I presented it in a webinar.

2.4   *The secrets of the other five Cello Suites*

In the following first months of 2022 I extended the analysis to the other Bach's Cello Suites finding the same hidden 3 voices canon in every piece, even in the unsuspected Prélude and Fugue of the 5th Suite, that had a double structure : it was both a Fugue *and* a double canon at the same time !

The way to build a canon was sometime different, so this discovery journey was full of surprises, and it was a pleasure to discover and listen to the new hidden effects. It was also interesting to notice that some small sections or singular notes were not compliant with the double canon, for instance in the Prélude of the first Suite: may be Bach had let a "hole" to be completed, or it was erased by some accident (water on the ink scores, mouses bites ?) and someone else (Anna Magdalena ?) found a reasonable melody to complete it.

In addition to this, I observed that in each Suite there was a unique piece that was working as 7 voices canon (being more tolerant with the parallel 4th and 5th), a different piece of each Suite, so that at the end the different pieces could be assembled in a hidden "seventh Suite for 7 Cellos".

The last piece of the last Suite was even working as 10 voices canon, I adapted it for a wind ensemble (to better hear the different voices associated to different instruments).

A researcher [6b] had proposed a thesis attributing all of the Cello Suites to Bach's wife, but after my research I considered that hearing and composing 3 voices (or more) hidden canons was like a signature of J.S. Bach that nobody could imitate. I will explain why in the second part of this book.

In the first attachment you can find the solo Cello Suites canons guide (with the start of each piece and the time shift between the voices). Some audio files are also linked to give a taste of the canons.

2.5   Discovering the Suites for other instruments

After having analysed 6x7 = 42 pieces in the Cello Suites it was now clear that J.S. Bach was a "serial canoner", he had a natural, spontaneous way of hearing and composing melodies with hidden canons, like a professional disease, for some mysterious reason to be unveiled.

To verify it, I had to inspect more pieces. Having in mind that the "travel Suite" was a must for the prince Leopold, in the first quarter of 2022 I extended the analysis to the other pieces that Bach was composing at his court for one melodic instrument played alone: the Violin and the Flute Suites.

Please keep in mind than when I lightly say "analyse a piece" it actually means patiently copying this music, note by note, on my computer, by hand, like J.S. Bach did when copying the music on paper, just with much less stress on doing errors, on making ink stains, on wasting precious paper and on getting punished for it! The further step is easier than the previous amanuensis work: it just consists in creating further voices, *copying and pasting* the first one, and finding the right *time shift* between the voices, checking that the added voice fits at least for 80% of his content with the other overlapped voices, getting a pleasant result. There is also another way to do this work in our modern times: you can search for a midi file version of the piece you want to analyse; you read/import it with a common music writing software and then you create the other voices copying and pasting as previously described. It is much faster indeed, but the pity doing it, is that the rhythmical content may completely change compared to the original scores. Furthermore, you are missing the pleasure to see the handwritten scores of the Bach's family/Company, and all of the small comments written there, as well as the discovery of eventual errors and discrepancies between several versions of the original ... you are missing the history!

To save time (in the Violin Suites there were a lot of notes to be copied compared to the Cello Suites), I only was searching directly for pieces belonging to the six solo Violin Partitas and Sonatas (BWV 1001-1006) that were working as 7 voices canon, to build a 7th hidden Suite for Violin as I had done for the Cello ones. I started by my preferred ones and I found it working well, one piece in each Partita and Sonata, a different piece in each Suite, so I stopped the work there.

For the musicology friends who want to continue my work, the other pieces of the Violin Suites are at your fully disposal to unveil and hear the triple canons for the first time after three centuries: I can ensure you that it's worth your time and effort!

Then I attacked the Partita BWV 1013 for solo Flute, the Allemande, Courante, Sarabande, Bourrée Anglaise revealed its hidden 4 voices canons. To "complete" the poor, unachieved Suite I looked at other Bach's famous pieces for Flute (like the *Prelude*, found in the BWV 846 and the *Badinerie* BWV 1067), finding out the same hidden canons. Probably J.S. Bach was reusing the original solo Flute material of this Suite for major pieces. I have to admit that the musical result of the pieces for Flute is less impressive and convincing than that of the Suites for the Cello or for Violin. This may explain why Bach was not satisfied with the BWV 1013 and disassembled it. To further complete the Suite, I recently analysed the *Gigue* from the Lute Suite BWV 997 that works as 5 voices canon and the famous *Siciliano* from the Sonata BWV 1031 that works as 7 voices canon.

At this point I had finished exploring the Suites for single voice instruments, the melodic ones. But listening to the Suites for keyboard, the French Suites (BWV 812-817) and the English Suites (BWV 806-811), I remarked that the density of notes was not such high considering a ten fingers instrument, so in the summer vacations of 2022 I analysed all of the starting sections of the Suites and found out the hidden multiple canons: all of these Suites can be played by 3 Harpsichords or Pianos. I also added the missed Préludes to the incomplete French Suites, taking it from the "spare" Préludes or Préludes and Fugues provided by J.S. Bach, that were also hiding 3 voices canons (BWV 935, BWV 934, BWV 925, BWV 876, BWV 816, BWV 937). The analysis of these Suites was teaching a lot to me, because they were not written in Köthen for the Prince Leopold: they were written before. Consequently, my initial assumption of "travel Suites for Leopold" was not the right one! Anyway, it must be noted that being able to animate a dance session with a single musician was still a great commercial idea for a score. I think the first ones were the French Suites without the Préludes. Probably the idea was to change each time of Prélude (or to improvise it!) before playing the dances, so Bach was preparing a lot of possible Préludes separately, in many different tonalities, for any eventuality.

2.6   Consequences on the way of playing the Suites

Actually, a musician after these discoveries can go on playing the Suites alone, in usual concert rooms, because Bach decided writing it like this. Now it may be played as well by three (or more) musicians in canon, or by one musician assisted by a sound system with artificial echoes, or by one musician placed in a special room with natural echoes (as it happened to me) to let a wider public discover this multiple canon novelty.

Concerning the interpretation of the Suites the musicians can go on as they prefer, more or less romantically, or with extreme manneristic styles, but they must be aware that now it is sure that *J.S. Bach was certainly not hearing it like this*. The presence of two additional immanent canon's voices is fully incompatible with the sudden tempo (speed) changes, or with too long stops between two phrases, or between two notes often used by manneristic interpreters. Be sure that *avoiding stops, adopting a stable, regular tempo, or performing only slow speed variations* is more compliant to the hidden canons and better respects the initial perspective.

It must be underlined that playing the Suites with several instruments in canon is a great exercise, because it requires a precise *control of the speed*, that we are not used to adopt while playing it alone as well as *an additional control of the loudness* of the different voices: my suggestion is to always keep the first voice louder and to decrease further and further the loudness when adding other voices, as it happens with natural echoes.

2.7   Eccentric excursus about the Numerology

Here I shall spend some words about the numerology and Bach's Suites; it is a matter that would merit to be better inquired than just through these few remarks. At J.S. Bach's time the Numerology was an important knowhow that everyone was using, more or less, willing or unwilling, to build her/his own mental habitudes and beliefs, like the superstitious ones, based on personal and collective agreements and rules.

Having a look on the complete list of the Suites composed by J.S. Bach (for instance in the official archive in Leipzig, but also in https://en.wikipedia.org/wiki/Suite_(Bach)), we immediately can remark that he composed several complete **sets** of 6 Suites: **one** set for Cello (BWV 1007-1012), **one** set for Violin (BWV 1001-1006), **four** sets for Harpsichord (BWV 806-811, BWV 812-817, BWV 825-830, BWV 818-824). In each Suite there were typically 6 dances. Please note that if the sets of Suites had been exactly 6, then we would have got the "devil's number" 666, which would be fully unacceptable for a champion of the music considered as Religion expression [9b], fortunately there are also some additional Suites and Overtures for Harpsichord (BWV 831, BWV 832-845), or Lute (BWV 995-998), or Orchestra (BWV 1066-1069-1070?), and some "spare" movements (mainly Preludes). Anyway, the grouping of the Suites for Harpsichord was done after his death, so keep calm and be sure *there was certainly no satanic intent from his side* and that you can forget this paragraph.

Just remember that J.S. Bach was the 7th child of 7 children of a splendid family who built a lost musical paradise around him, before collapsing. His music education was done at the St. Michael's Church in Ohrdruf and at the St. Michael's School in Lüneburg, now St. Michael is the angel in charge to play the 1^{rst} of the 7 Trumpets at the Apocalypse. Consequentially he should have got a positive relationship with the number 7. Even more important: in the western culture 7 is mostly considered a "happy number" associated to the 7th resting day, moreover it is the number that represents the *achievement of a creation cycle* (the holy creation week in the Bible), while the number 6 represents an incomplete creation. This may explain why in the Cello Suites and in many others, Bach added a Prélude before the dances to get a 7th movement following Marin Marais example. Moreover, to complete the French Suites and the other ones like the Partitas there are a lot of "spare" Préludes, or Préludes and Fugue, including those of the Well-tempered Clavier. As already recalled the Prélude was not only a musical introduction preparing to the particular style and ambiance of the other dances of a given Suite, but also a way to entertain the public of a court waiting for the main ludic dancing time with a more impressive and virtuous piece, just to be listened. Anyway the "7th hidden Suite" for Cello described above and the same for Violin are also "correcting" the incomplete number of 6 Suites for each set. Concerning the four sets of Suites for Harpsichord I think that there is no need for searching for the pieces hiding more complex (for instance 7 voices) canons, because finding a 7th Suite to each set can be done just associating one of the Spurious Suites.

2.8 *Extending the analysis to other masterpieces*

Following the above Suites list and remarks, many other hidden 3 voices canons should be discovered by the sceptic readers in the Partitas and in the other Suites for Harpsichord and in those for Lute, I didn't explore it: I'm keeping some amusement for an eventual retirement!

To assess if the 3 voices canon was like a systematic hidden composing ingredient of J.S. Bach, not limited to the solo instruments Suites, I finally analysed some Concertos. I found out that

1) in the Concerto for Violin BWV 1041 the solo Violin voice hides a 3 voices canon, i.e. it can be played with 3 soloists!

2) in the Concerto for two Violins BWV 1043 both of the solo Violin's voices hide a 4 voices canon, i.e. it can be played with 8 soloists!

3) in the Concerto for Oboe and Violin BWV 1060R each of the solo voices hides a 4 voices canon structure, i.e., it can be played with 8 soloists, 4 Violins and 4 Oboes! In addition to this also the 4 strings of the orchestra in the first movement seems to work as 4 voices canons, such that 4 orchestra can play there...

4) in the 5th Brandenburger, finding out that for the Allegro the solo parts for Flute and Violin are all composed to be compliant with hidden 4 voices canons, i.e., it can be played with 4 solo Violins and 4 solo Flutes. Actually, I wasn't able to find hidden canons in the other movements of the 5th Brandenburger:
   a) may be J.S. Bach wasn't composing the hidden canons if he hadn't time, or if he was delegating his wife, or some of his sons and daughters, to complete a work, without asking them to put double canons in it.
   b) this demonstrates in any case that the contrapuntal way of composing doesn't imply at all the possibility to find a several voices hidden canon!

All of the scores of these researches are freely available on the websites IMSLP (see the "arrangements", or the "other" sections) and AIMAmusic (https://aimamusic.it/nuova-musica/).

2.9 *Contrapuntal objections*

Several musicians told me that finding canons was an obvious and natural thing in a contrapuntal composition: this objection may be true for two voices canons (but I don't think that it is true for any contrapuntal piece), or for simple melodies with an oscillating and repeated shape, as the one shown in BWV 1072, but it is really wrong when looking for 3 voices (or more) canons and when the melodies are complex, or are changing in an incompatible way, like the "wrong sections" of the second Cello Suite, or the not working movements of the 5th Brandenburger, while keeping a contrapuntal style. If you still are not convinced, please try composing 3 voices canons, or look for hidden ones in other authors works, that used to compose contrapuntal pieces!

The next chapter will give more insight in the complexity of Bach's hidden canons.

3   The difficulty of composing multiple canons

3.1 *What is a canon?*

The canon, in a musical sense is an interesting way of accompanying a melody using as second voice the same melody delayed in the time. In a symbolic way, the canon represents the different generations who cohabit and coexist bearing and dying one after the other. The canon is often/always used in a never-ending circular form, repeating the melody as soon it ends; this makes audible the Greek "panta rei" concept of circular repetition of the story.

From the composer practical point of view, each element of the melody is composed to be pleasantly overlapped with the element coming just before and with the element coming just after. In the folk songs we often find a very simplified form of canon, where the elements of the melody are repeated or alternated, so that an element has just to be compatible with another one. The graphic representation of these **"trivial canons"** can be done with coloured segments on the time line, as follows:

Figure 7a: trivial canon with alternated elements

Figure 7b: trivial canon with repeated elements

One can remark that these trivial canons can work overlapping more voices, but the in the Fig.7a case the third voice would coincide with the first one, in the Fig.7b case (repeated elements) the fifth voice would coincide with the first one. The overlapped elements are always the same and this kind of music is gooey and mostly used to be sung by children. However, the effect of overlapping a melody with itself creates a new sensation and pleasure.

We also can find **"evolutive canons"**, where the elements are changing continuously, each element is never repeated. In this form each element shall be pleasantly *compliant both with the previous and with the following element*. The graphic representation of it can be the following one:

Figure 8: simple evolutive canon with changing elements

This kind of canon is more interesting and avoids gooey repetitions.

3.2   The multiple canons

Starting with 3 voices canons the complexity drastically increases and almost nobody can hear and understand in advance if a melody one is composing will satisfy the 3 voices canon rules: each element shall be *compliant with 3 <u>couples</u> of two preceding elements and of two following elements.*

Figure 9: double evolutive canon (3 voices)

The higher the number of voices increases, the more complex the problem becomes and the composer requires a much deeper study for each composed element: for a n voices evolutive canon each element shall be compliant with 2(n-1) elements, at the same time with n-1 of them. For instance, for a 5 voices canon each element of the melody must be compatible with 8 elements (4 before it and 4 after it), actually with *5 different quartets of elements*, look at the black element in the following scheme:

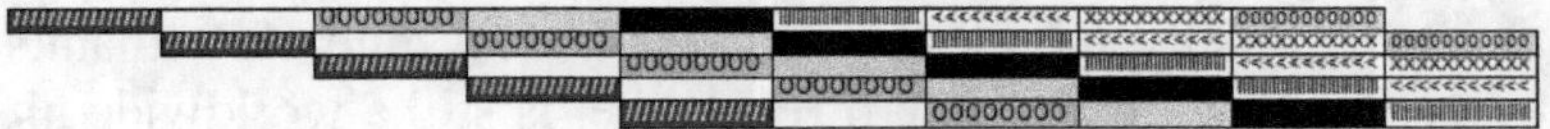

Figure 10: 5 voices evolutive canon

Now you can better understand why it was and still it is difficult for me finding a proper solution for the missed sections of the 3 voices canon in the Prélude of the second Cello Suite. You can understand as well that realizing the 8 voices canon represented in Fig.1, as Bach did in the last piece of the last Cello Suite, is not an easy task, and doing it while creating a pleasant melody is a real masterpiece, even in the computer's time. The hidden multiple canons compatibility fully explains the particular style of J.S. Bach's melodies, that everyone can notice comparing it to those of the other composers and that was quite mysterious to me before the present discovery.

3.3   *Main Canons context in the times of J.S. Bach*

To get consistent scientific information, please refer to Denis Collins detailed work [1] and [4]. Let me do just a couple of remarks here. Considering the poor context of J.S. Bach in the years spent in Ohrdruf hosted by his brother Johann Christoph, organist, with few scores to be intensively copied and learnt, it seems difficult that J.S.B. could discover pieces like the *Ricercari, canone e sonate per 2 violoncelli* (1689) of Domenico Gabrielli, that were evolutive canons in the simplest form, alternating an element of melody with an element of accompaniment and simplifying the compatibility in an analogous way to Fig. 4. On the contrary, it is sure in a German context that Bach was knowing and learning the famous *Canon and Giga in D major*, (1680, P.37) of Johann Pachelbel, who had been teaching his brother: this piece has got an ostinato bass line and three voices of a simplified form of evolutive canon, where the voices are alternating a phrase and its variations/accompaniments, the elements are long but always the same tonality and the harmony is poor. In spite of, or thanks to its simplicity, the Canon of Pachelbel is still a worldwide hit and was certainly a beautiful discovery and a reference for the young Bach.

3.4   *J.S. Bach's evolutive and modulating canons*

Both of the previous pieces keep the same tonality, for their begin to their end. On the contrary, the evolutive canons created by J.S. Bach require a higher degree of compatibility between two adjacent elements each one being possibly in a different tonality (modulating melody). The 3 voices evolutive canons are already difficult to be composed, as previously explained, but a true genie and talent is required when changing of the tonality in the melody and mixing three elements of different tonalities while keeping a pleasant result at the end. Probably Bach was learning how to easily change of tonality during the precious months spent in the free imperial city of Lübeck, thanks to a 400 km long walk, spying the famous organist and improviser Dieterich Buxtehude with his stylus phantasticus, Preludes and Fugues.

Of course, the crab-canons, or the reflected ones, or the "per augmentationem or diminutionem" ones found in BWV 1087 are far more complex from a theoretical point of view, but on another side, they also can no longer be clearly heard and perceived, nor fully enjoyed without a visual support.

Anyway, the main study of this book is dedicated to audible modulating multiple evolutive canons.

4 Comments on the attached "canons guides"

4.1 The short canons guide

In the attached scores you can find all of starts with the canons time shifts of the different pieces of the Cello Suites, of some of the Violin Suites, of the unachieved Flute Suite, of the French Suites and English Suites for Harpsichord, including some Préludes that had the same tonality of the French Suites missing it and also the starts of the Concertos I have explored. The complete canon scores of the Cello Suites, the Violin Suites and Flute Suite are freely available on the web sites IMSLP and AIMAmusic, but the previous "Guides" with only the *pieces starts* are a better tool (and it saves a lot of paper and trees), because each player can keep her/his preferred/usual scores edition and just apply the time delay when playing it with other performers. A different sense can be found in the "corrected" Cello Suites pieces and in the different arrangements for different instruments (mainly Cello-Viola-Violin trios, or entire wind ensemble when there was a 7 to 10 voices canon) to let better hear the canon structure. For the Cello Suites, as explained previously I spent a lot of time finding "corrections" of single notes, or of entire sections (for the second Cello Suite); honestly I would now avoid this work, because it makes no sense in a mere musicology discovery of canons and it doesn't pretend, on another hand, to be an artistic work, as the result is always unsatisfying compared to the original solo voice work, even in the case of sections that were visibly "fixed" in a wrong way, probably not written by J.S. Bach.

4.2 *Surprising hidden Ragtime rhythms*

The rhythmical complexity that can be observed in some pieces and heard in the audio samples reported in the links is the most controversial and surprising side of these 3 voices canons. From a detractor's side it can be described as a trivial trick to escape from having stable chords of dissonant notes, because the notes are finely shifted in the time, and it can be seen as an expedient to get a 3 voices canon where there is no one. But having searched for these canons for a long time and tried many possible combinations I can assure you that this kind of "trick" doesn't work at all for other pieces where there is really no hidden canon (see for instance the other movements of the Brandeburger), it simply creates confusion. Moreover, the basic rhythmical complexity can be found in the BWV 1072 canon archetype as well. The consequence of this is that these immanent rhythms, typical of later romantic rhapsodies, were indeed heard by J.S. Bach, but were very/too modern for Bach's time and too destabilizing as dancing base: we have to wait till the Ragtime's era to find something similar in a dancing room!

4.3 *The church ambiance when listening the multiple canons*

Excepted for the previous pieces with a funny rhythmical effect, the other pieces analysed there and that can be listened in the linked files, create a sort of church sound, full of resonating elements. When listening it for a too long time, because of the increased attention required for its complexity, it becomes tiring. This also explains why Bach was not proposing the explicit canonized pieces to be played for several instruments (in spite of potentially selling longer scores and getting 3 times more money!): it would be for sure less appreciated than the solo instrument ones. Why then composing such complex multiple canons and keeping it hidden? The second part of this booklet just tries to give an answer to this question.

PART II UNDERSTANDING is better than UNDERLAYING

5 Necessity is the mother of wit

It is now time to try to understand why J.S. Bach was composing in this particular way and why he was so proud of it, to choose

Fig.11 Johann Sebastian Bach (aged 61) in a portrait by Elias Gottlob Haussmann, second version of his 1746 canvas. Bach is holding a copy of the six-part canon BWV 1076
http://www.jsbach.net/bass/elements/bach-hausmann.jpg , Public Domain, https://commons.wikimedia.org/w/index.php?curid=1270015

to keep in his Portrait a paper with a multiple canon as summa of the work of his life.

His Monogram (seal) too has a crown on it: he was aware of being (and *is* indeed forever) the King of the Canons. More precisely we can observe a series of three lines recalling the three voices canons, mirrored to, may be, suggest to further search for three voices crab canons hidden somewhere …

Fig.12 Bach's seal (centre), used throughout his Leipzig years. It contains the superimposed letters J S B in mirror image topped with a crown. The flanking letters illustrate the arrangement on the seal.
https://commons.wikimedia.org/wiki/File:Bach_Seal.svg#filelinks Public Domain.

5.1 *Bach's harsh life*

One cannot be proud of a talent one is born with, but if one has developed this talent by hard exercises and hard life, then one really can be.

Johann Sebastian was the last of seven children and was surely pampered by his parents, brothers, sisters and taught by musician uncles, playing on many music instruments, from the Violin to the Harpsichord, he was growing carefree in a small town of the Holy Roman Empire. He was just 9 years old when his mother died and some months later his father wasn't able to survive to this family collapse. The previous paradise was lost forever. His eldest brother Johann Christoph had a work as organist at the St. Michael's church in Ohrdruf and hosted him as well as another young brother. The school wasn't a safe place for him ([13]). We only can imagine that in this new life with J.S. was taking refuge in the church and intensively learning playing organ from his brother to become a musician too. Surely, he was copying all of the available/lend music scores to discover some south German composers' work and learning how to write and to play music, however any copying error that was wasting the highly precious paper was surely punished. He was clever and brilliant: he was chosen and financed to be further educated in the famous St. Michael's School in Lüneburg. The point here is that he was surely spending a lot of time alone, playing organ in the church and solving in this way any autistic reaction trend to the orphanage status.

5.2   *The Room Acoustics context as root-cause*

In the time and the country of J.S. Bach, the music was mostly performed in the bare, austere Lutheran temples, or in wide empty rooms with stoned walls of the court's palaces with a few of tapestry. From an acoustics point of view, both of these spaces were characterized by a long reverberation time and some dominant echo, generally two in the Hall churches, where the height is the same everywhere and there is no distinction between nave and aisles, corresponding to the widest sizes of the room (typically the nave length and the constant height). The result was certainly an acoustical chaos and a very difficult listening of music and speeches, especially at a distance larger than 2 or 3 meters from the players/speakers. The acoustically better alternative were cloisters, yards and public squares, but the German weather was limiting the use of such places to the short warm season. The taverns were just suitable places for minstrels and no composer was considering it. In the baroque churches on the contrary, because of the various shapes, chapels, niches, statues, columns and the countless stuccoes acting as natural sound diffusers at least the echoes problem was probably mitigated and a genie like Bach would not have had such problems to think about. Nowadays one would simply treat the church/temple with thick sound-absorbing panels on the walls corresponding to the widest sizes.

However, the young J.S. Bach was spending his life on the organ of the temple in Ohrdruf (a Hall church = Hallenkirche), his main acoustical problem was to get a clear, sharp music, fighting against the overall rumbles, the disharmonious overlaps, the sound disorder, the confusion that was incompatible with the pure and tidy concept of order and harmony of his Religion, of the Leibniz's philosophy and of his personal belief. The same happened in the time spent in Weimar in the ducal palace rooms and in the castle church.

5.3 Bach's genial solution

After having found so many 3 voices canons in Bach's work, I came to the **thesis** that the genial solution found by the young Johann Sebastian to solve the acoustical problem of the echoes in the rooms where he was playing, was to *adapt his music in order to get a pleasant overlap with the echoes*, a sort of synergy with the first emitted sound *to stand out of the confuse reverberant part of the sound*, so called reverberant background.

To allow this finding **two exceptional gifts were necessary.** Firstly, a talent to adapt his own playing to exterior events, also called *trained improvisation:* the intense desire to freely improvise was a gift provided by the boredom, once the few scores available at the brother's home were extensively explored and exploited. Secondly an *outstanding development of the hearing*, with a maniacal/autistic attention paid to the echoes and to the global effect of the music in a room and not only to the few notes played at a given moment. This discerning hearing found the perfect occasion to be developed in the church of Ohrdruf: a gift of the loneliness and of the silence.

The famous improvisation of J.S. Bach is the result of his ability to *imagine* new melodies and of his extreme *control* of each played element, in order to get it compatible with the previous one coming back with the echoes, and with the next one. This execution method corresponds to the evolutive canon's essence. The two echoes of the Hallenkirchen imply playing 3 voices canons.

Time and space. When analysing the canons hidden in the different Suites of J.S. Bach (the French and English ones, those for Cello, violin and flute) one finds that the time shift can vary from a quarter of second to half a second, this corresponds to a nave length about 40 - 80 meters. Among the first organ pieces he wrote, for instance, the Fugue in C BWV Anh.107 or the Fantasia in C major, BWV 570 are also canons. This supports quite well my following theory: I suppose that *the ear training and the first improvisation steps happened in Ohrdruf, while the conscientious elaboration and the technical refinement came in the following studying and first working years*. I didn't analyse yet the works of Dieterich Buxtehude, that Bach was spying in Lübeck, and who was intensively using fugued structures, but I don't think that such hidden canons are present in it, the immanent (hidden) canons are certainly a J.S. Bach invention, based on his own life journey. This performing technique based on canons, fully explains J.S. Bach success in the improvisation competitions: he was hearing the sound coming back when choosing the next notes to be played. The use of the hidden multiple canons becomes a *secret ingredient* in the compositions of J.S. Bach and he was trying teaching it to his children, as one can see in the BWV 1072-86 and 1087. This assumption that

Bach wanted to achieve an acoustical effect of clean and sharp music hearing in diffuse fields with echoes using hidden canons was "validated" personally when listening at an organ concert in a large church: only the pieces of Bach were clear and outstanding, the other composer's pieces were just merged in the overall rumble.

As additional argument for the previous thesis I recall that Bach showed a high **interest for the echo's** phenomenon: several of his compositions are named Echo (in BVW 821, 831, 1002). To be noted: the interest for the echoes and its use in musical works is much older and documented at least from the Renaissance time (H. Vecchi, A. Banchieri, G. Gabrieli...), nearer to Bach's time there were I. Posch, G. Scronx (Echo in F major 1617), S. Scheidt (Echo ad manuale duplex 1624), C. de Tallard (Air in Echo, Suite pour Lute) and later A. Lotti (Sonata a 4: Echo-Adagio-Presto 1717), A. Vivaldi (RV552, Concerto con violino principale con altro per eco 1740) and dozens of later composers in the music history, but you see that Bach is the King of them all.

For a long time, J.S. Bach attempted to **add some bells on the organ** in Mühlhausen, when he was in charge to follow its construction and tuning. This idea is very surprising: not only the organ is reach in keyboards, but also in different registers, this means that many timbers and sounds are already available. The idea came from the organ in Arnstadt with its Cymbelstern, but differently from the Cymbelstern, that was just rotating and automatically and chaotically moving the bells with the organ tubes air outlet, Bach wanted to create a manually controlled set of bells, impacted by some hammers, controlled by the keyboard, like in a harpsichord. In my interpretation, the scope was to get a very different sound from the organ ones with a *very short start* due to the hammer impact, in order to be identified and better heard and to precisely know the time interval of the echoes, necessary to find the right tempo for the canon's improvisations.

Now a **taste of fussiness**: the scientific objection to this thesis could be that the different echoes are generally not coming back at a regular time interval, especially if the sizes of the room or the distance between the sound source and the walls are not the right ones. I only can suppose that in the church of Ohrdruf the position of the organ and the sizes were the right ones: for instance, if the organ was at the end of the nave, and the nave was twice long as the church height, then the echoes were due to the same room sizes and came back with a constant time delay to his ears.

Let me do a last fussy remark: the serial composing of masterpieces with hidden canons clearly belongs to the **time spent in Weimar** (1708-1717), so I presume that Bach was facing there echo problems similar to the Ohrdruf church's ones also in the music rooms of the ducal palace, because most of the pieces I did analyse are composed for "chamber music" rather than for church's one. Bach's organ work should better be analysed to find hidden canons in order to confirm my thesis, if nothing is found it would mean that the intuition on how using hidden canons was not related to the Ohrdruf's church time but to the Weimar's one. Which would be more effective from an acoustics point of view, since one can choose the right place where to play in a palace concert room and this cannot be done with a church's organ.

6 Acoustical and psycho-acoustical effects

6.1 *The acoustical memory*

Following to the psycho-acoustics basic concepts, the acoustical memory of normal peoples is very short, especially when listening to mindless noises: for instance, when comparing the noise of two different vehicle setups in the car industry, the tests shall occur in the shortest time frame if ever two twin vehicles are available at the same time, or the comparison shall be done based on sound recordings to be re-listened using headphones. For other sounds related to the human survival, thanks to the physiologic evolution, the hearing is instinctively much more sensitive, so small variations appearing in a usual noise of the surrounding nature, like the low-level noise of a mosquito, a sudden silence, a leaf cracking, or the dysfunction of a usual machine can be immediately detected. More generally when an emotion, or an important information is associated to listening, like it happens for a speech, the brain is more precise and attentive. Speaking about trained hearing, musicians mainly have no problems distinguishing 24th of octave intervals (quarters of tones), or remembering a melody, or a more complex music piece in terms of frequency intervals (harmony) and for some absolute hears also in terms of absolute frequency values, and also in terms of sound loudness for a time about one hour, allowing them to give a dynamic to their music interpretation, using forte, piano, crescendo and so on. They also can remember hours of music. Actors can remember poetry, or entire theatre pieces, many religious persons can remember an entire sacred book.

On another side we must remark that most of normal untrained people can remember melodies, or short poetry pieces, or usual phrases, especially just after having heard it, because *the interpretation of the listened noise takes some time*, for instance for the spoken language, especially when different persons are speaking at the same time and all of them have to be understood. In other words, the useful sound is "kept alive" in the brain for a given time, like the sound in a resonant chamber, a sort of *interpretation buffer*. Coming back to Bach's country, it must be observed (like Charlie Chaplin pleasantly in "the great dictator" did!) that the long suspended German phrasal structures may take an accomplished sense just at their end and consequently require a longer remembering time. This systematic and unconscious elaboration time in our brain exists for the music as well: this means that *while listening to a new sound the previous listened sound coexists in our memory*.

6.2 *Bach's second intuition*

I believe that J.S. Bach had observed and understood it in his Ohrdruf time, where Ohr means hear and Ruf means call, so it was the ideal vocation place for Bach's hearing! In my assumption he was bringing to a conscious and controlled state a phenomenon that was unconscious for other people and he was using it to win his improvisation competitions and to get extraordinary effects and sensations *in the listeners brains*, where *the music is accompanying and enriching itself,* thanks to the temporary memory (buffer).

This acoustical memory effect doesn't depend on the physical presence of echoes in the room, so it concerns the usual listening experience. This second part of my thesis could then be considered as an alternative to the first one: no echoes problems to be solved, no room acoustics, just brain psycho-acoustics matters and Bach's intuition.

I prefer to believe that both explanations can coexist, as I like both. I experienced personally the physical one (room acoustics) and the second one (psycho-acoustics) is theoretically harder to be demonstrated, but you can try doing it by yourself, just concentrating on what you hear and remember while listening to Bach's pieces. Anyway, even considering this psychic effect explanation alone, the indication to keep a stable tempo when playing Bach's music, or to perform only slow speed variations, remains valid.

6.3   The strategy beyond the hidden Canons

When discovering firstly the hidden 3 to 7 voices canons in the solo instrument Suites (for Cello, Violin or Flute), I thought that it was a genial strategy of Bach to get a polyphonic concert effect with a single instrument, especially useful for the travelling times with the Prince Leopold of Köthen, to minimize the musicians necessary for a performance. This was probably a "side effect", I still didn't know at this time that J.S. Bach had already composed a lot of hidden canons pieces in the previous "jobs" in Weimar: the English Suites and the French Suites for harpsichord! Moreover, he would keep composing like this also for larger formations: many Concertos for orchestra and solo instruments contain hidden 3 voices canons! Hence, there was clearly no need to artificially improve the effect of a single instrument just for a travelling function.

These later discoveries let me elaborating the above thesis, on the clarity effect in bad music chambers (room-acoustical effect) and of the enriched sensation in the human brain (psycho-acoustical effect) obtained by this way of composing.

6.4   Why hidden for such a long time?

The solo instrument Suites are the pieces where one can discover the hidden canons in the easiest way; I did it as cello player, but also thanks to my autistic stubbornness (splendid consonant canons in this word!), that made me insist, after many years, thanks to my uncle's passion for the analysis of texts and philosophical contexts, to my father's studies on Religions and psychology, to the Acoustics doctorate, to the metamusical composing method [11], thanks to all of these ingredients that together allowed me to think the phaenomena and to find an explanation: the outcome, the result of the research was driving my entire improbable life journey. The Calvinist Prince Leopold would speak about predestination and necessary universe.

But why did nobody remark these hidden canons in the past 3 centuries? Let me try to find some explanation: the Suites of dances were a musical form that no longer was in use after Bach's time, the ephemeral dances used in the courts changed quite soon, the Suites were old and useless, the following romantic music for solo instruments was mostly played in smaller bourgeois rooms without echoes and lastly Bach's Suites were too complex and the scores too expansive for the folk music players.

However, the Suites of Bach were actually studied by great composers like Mendelssohn, and the work of Bach has influenced Haydn, Mozart, Beethoven and the following composers, but nobody took care about the refined canons in spite of Bach's portrait-legacy. The fugues seemed to be more complex and interesting to musicology. This also means that his wife and sons didn't tell anybody about the "secret ingredient" of the Bach composing company in spite of their bad economic conditions: they must have sworn about keeping it, or they were completely unaware ...

Even in our late romantic time the soloists like Casals, or Glenn Gould, spent their life playing the Suites, however they preferred exploiting the beauty of the Suites to get more success without taking care of the hidden treasures. On another side, it is difficult indeed to coldly analyse such beautiful pieces, where the melodies are fascinating, changing every time, adopting very different styles and effects and distracting you from thinking that it can be a canon.

6.5 *Last revision of the Suites*

After having formulated the physical explanation of the game with the echoes, I questioned my first analyzes on the Cello

Suites: the delays of the voices in time were too long compared to the Suites that I analyzed later. I have thus found solutions with shorter delays which do not impose any changes in the Preludes of the second Suite and the first Suite. All of the assumptions on the "holes" left in the scores and completed by Anna Magdalena, in paragraphs 2.5 and 2.6, although seductive and amusing, are no longer needed with these new solutions. The start of the second Suite becomes then:

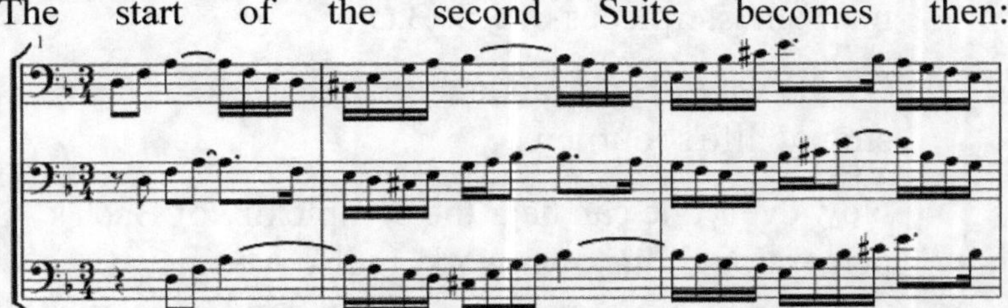

All this work would therefore have arisen from my incorrect listening to the Prelude of the 2nd Suite, done according to the habits of singing canons with delays of about one bar: a fruitful error in any case, without which the true canons would not have come back to light. I have re-analysed various pieces and posted the new versions of the scores on the IMSLP and AIMAmusic sites. It should also be noted that the short delays between the voices limit the overlaps between different tonalities to shorter segments of music and facilitate the composition of multiple evolutive and modulating canons. There is nothing intuitive about listening to short delays, it is difficult and brings out the exceptional nature of J.S. Bach's hearing.

7 Conclusions

1. I 've found a hidden treasure following the living map of a music score, after three centuries of the composer's patience: precious and beautiful multiple voices evolutive and modulating canons are immanently set, like diamonds and emeralds, in many masterpieces of J.S. Bach.

2. By the way I better understood the sense of my strange life's journey.

3. Now everyone can hear the complexity of Bach's perception of his own work, rediscover his masterpieces and experience new brain capacities.

4. Musicians can play together, or alone with some device's help, and discover new ways of interpreting classic works. Cloning musicians makes finally some sense!

5. They can take more care when choosing the position where to play and listening to Bach's music in a bad room.

6. Musicologists can further research and discover unexpected worlds in Bach's scores, or waste some time disputing about my work, if they like.

7. And if it was just a dream, it was a beautiful one, worth to be dreamed indeed!

HIDDEN CANONS SCORES REFERENCES

[A] Cello Suites https://imslp.org/wiki/File:PMLP4291-6CelloSuitesHiddenCanonsGuide.pdf

[B] Violin Suites best of
https://imslp.org/wiki/Special:ImagefromIndex/790271/vg25

[C] "completed" Flute Suite
https://imslp.org/wiki/Special:ImagefromIndex/788474/vg25

[D] "completed" French Suites
https://imslp.org/wiki/Special:ImagefromIndex/809911/vg25

[E] English Suites
https://imslp.org/wiki/Special:ImagefromIndex/809741/vg25

[F] Goldberg Variations Aria
https://imslp.org/wiki/Special:ImagefromIndex/809278/vg25

[G] Violin Concerto BWV 1041
https://imslp.org/wiki/Special:ImagefromIndex/821336/vg25

[H] 2 Violins Concerto BWV 1043
https://imslp.org/wiki/Special:ImagefromIndex/821337/vg25

[I] Oboe and Violin Concerto BWV 1060R
https://imslp.org/wiki/Special:ImagefromIndex/821335/vg25

[J] 5th Brandenburger BWV 1050 Allegro
https://imslp.org/wiki/Special:ImagefromIndex/822690/vg25

LISTENING samples on YouTube (and other)

https://www.youtube.com/channel/UCG4BI8Q1vR7SbMxCxDJ_yIA

https://metamusica.altervista.org/

Basic Bibliography

[1.a] Denis Collins, *From Bull to Bach: In Search of Precedents for the "Complete" Version of the Canon by Augmentation and Contrary Motion in J. S. Bach's "Musical Offering"* Source: Bach, Vol. 38, No. 2 (2007), pp. 39-63 Published by: Riemenschneider Bach Institute.

[1.b] Dennis Collins and W. Andrew Schloss, *An Unusual Effect in the Canon Per Tonos from J. S. Bach's Musical Offering* Source: Music Perception: An Interdisciplinary Journal, Vol. 19, No. 2 (Winter 2001), pp. 141-153 Published by: University of California Press

[1.c] Denis Collins, *Bach and Approaches to Canonic Composition in Early Eighteenth-Century Theoretical and Chamber Music Sources.* Source: Bach, Vol. 30, No. 2 (1999), pp. 27-48 Published by: Riemenschneider Bach Institute

[2] Marcel Bitsch , *J.S. Bach, canons BWV 1087: analyse et commentaires* 1977, Durand, T. Presse

[3] Christoph Wolff, "Bach's Handexemplar of the Goldberg Variations: A New Source", Journal of the American Musicological Society XXIV/2 (Summer 1976), pp. 224-241.

[4] Denis Collins *Historical precedents for Bach's "evolutio" canon BWV1087/10* Source: Bach, vol. 24, No. 1 (Spring-Summer, 1993), pp. 5-14 Published by: Riemenschneider Bach Institute

[5] Alexander Maykapar, September 2, 2015 THE 13th CANON: Portrait of J.S. Bach In https://www.projectawe.org/blog?category=AWE https://www.projectawe.org/blog?category=maria+danova

[6a] Athanase Papadopoulos, Mathématiques *et musique chez J.S. Bach*, 2000, L'ouvert 100, papadopoulos@math.u-strasbg.fr

[6b] Martin Jarvis, *Written by Mrs Bach,* 2011, HarperCollins Publishers Australia. http://www.harpercollins.com.au/9780733328725/

[7] Tony Phillips, *Math and the Musical Offering,* https://www.ams.org/publicoutreach/feature-column/fcarc-canons

[8] J.S. Bach Crab Canon on a Moebius band
https://www.openculture.com/2009/09/how_a_bach_canon_works.html

[9a] Denis Collins, *Bach's Occasional Canon BWV 1073 and "Stacked" Canonic Procedure in the Eighteenth Century* Source: Bach, Vol. 33, No. 2 (2002), pp. 15-34 Published by: Riemenschneider Bach Institute

[9b] Albert Clement, *Johann Sebastian Bach and the praise of God, some thoughts on the canon triplex (BWV 1076),* In: Music and theology: essays in honor of Robin A. Leaver/ed. by Daniel Zager-Lanham, Md.[u.a.], 2007.- S. 147-168

[10] Dr. Timothy A. Smith, Northern Arizona University *Canons and Fugues of J.S. Bach*, Tutorial 2020-2021

[11] https://metamusica.altervista.org/spiegazioni/generalinfo.html

[12] Bob van Asperen, contrib. F. Huneau, M. Quagliozzi, *François Dieupart's Biography Revised and the Genesis and Dating of his Six Suittes de Clavessin, with Remarks on their Influence on J.S. Bach*. Amsterdam, 2021

[13] John Eliot Gardiner, *Bach: Music in the Castle of Heaven,* 2013

About the author

Giovanni Pietro Orefice (Milano 1967-Gap-Grenoble-Lyon-Berlin-Paris-Torino-Milano/Desenzano/Modena), PhD in Acoustics, Cellist, Composer of Metamusic. See [11].

Die Geheimnisse der verborgenen Kanons von J.S. Bach

Büchlein für Johann Sebastian

Einführung

Wenn man die Musik des großen Komponisten J.S. Bach hört, kann jeder einen tiefen Nachhall seiner Melodien in seiner Seele spüren. Und wenn man seine Orgelmeisterwerke in einer halligen Kirche mit denen anderer Komponisten vergleicht, treten seine in auffallender Klarheit hervor. In diesem kleinen Buch werde ich versuchen, diese beiden Erfahrungen zu vertiefen und zu erläutern, und zwar auf der Grundlage der Untersuchungen, die ich vor kurzem getätigt habe, um die verborgenen Kanons in vielen berühmten Stücken von J.S. Bach aufzudecken. Diese Untersuchungen werde ich als Erstes darstellen. Ich habe mich bemüht, diesen Text einfach und verständlich zu schreiben und Fachausdrücke zu vermeiden. Er soll Musiker und Musikwissenschaftler inspirieren, indem er ihnen viele Anhaltspunkte für wissenschaftiche Forschungen liefert, und er soll ein Leitfaden für alle Liebhaber Bachs Musik sein, die in den Links angegebenen Stücken die Schönheit der mehrstimmigen Kanons entdecken und eine Erklärung für die unbeschreiblichen Gefühle bekommen, die sie beim Hören seiner Werke empfinden.

Entgegen allen Erwartungen, birgt J.S. Bachs Werk, selbst drei Jahrhunderte nach seiner Komposition, noch viele verborgene Schätze und Überraschungen. Der erste Teil dieses Büchleins stellt die umfangreichen musikwissenschaftlichen Forschungen vor, die ich zu dem grossartigen J.S. Bach durchgeführt habe, um die in seinem Werk verborgene, bisher unbekannte, immanente multiple Kanonstruktur zu enthüllen. Als Cellist, begann ich diese Entdeckung mit den Suiten für Violoncello solo; ich fuhr fort mit den Sonaten und Partiten für Violine, mit der unvollständigen Suite für Flöte, mit den Französischen und Englischen Suiten für Cembalo, fügte einige Präludien hinzu, um sie zu vervollständigen, und schloss mit der Untersuchung einiger Konzerte und Doppelkonzerte ab. In diesem Prozess möchte ich unerwartete rhythmische Effekte und unvollendete/fehlende Teile in einigen Stücken hervorheben, einige Hinweise zu ihrer Vervollständigung geben und einige Lösungen für alte Streitigkeiten und Zuordnungsprobleme anbieten. Ich werde versuchen zu erklären, wie schwierig es ist mehrstimmige Kanons zu komponieren und werde Vergleiche mit Stücken anderer berühmter Komponisten der Zeit anstellen, um ein neues Licht auf J.S. Bachs immer noch unterschätztes Talent und ungewöhnliche Fähigkeiten zu werfen.

Im zweiten Teil des Buches stelle ich eine innovative These vor, die das Wissen über akustische Physik und Psychoakustik aus meinem Studium und Beruf mit meinen Erfahrungen und Überlegungen als aktiver Musiker verbindet. Dieser ausergewöhnliche Ansatz bietet eine Erklärung für die praktische und taktische Motive die Bach hatte, mehrstimmige Kanons in seinen Melodien zu verstecken.

Diese Theorie erklärt uns, wie Bach als Improvisator und Komponist einige akustische Probleme beseitigte, und wie er sich damit einen Wettbewerbsvorteil in seinen ruhmreichen Improvisationsturnieren verschaffte. Die These besagt auch, dass Bach bestimmte psychoakustische Effekte instinktiv erkannte und sie sich als Geheimrezept zu eigen machte, um Meisterwerke zu komponieren und unsterbliche weltweite Anerkennung zu erzielen.

Wenn Sie sich nicht mit den Strukturen und der Entdeckung der versteckten Kanons auseinander setzen wollen, dann springen Sie zu Teil 2, Kapitel 5.

TEIL I KANONS, keine KANONEN

1 Explizite vs. versteckte, immanente Kanons

Einzelheiten über die Entdeckung verborgener Kanons finden Sie in Kapitel 2. Der Zweck dieses Kapitels ist die Unterscheidung zwischen den expliziten, sichtbaren Kanons in Bachs Kompositionen und den versteckten Kanons, die im zweiten Kapitel behandelt werden.

Übliche Sicht auf J.S. Bachs Kanons

Bachs bekannteste und am weitesten entwickelte Kanons sind die zehn explizit geschriebenen im *Musikalischen Opfer* BWV 1079 für den König von Preußen, vgl. [1], von denen Anton von Webern 1935 das *Ricercare für 6 Stimmen* orchestrierte. Auch die *Kanonvariation über Von Himmel hoch* (für Orgel) BWV 769 schrieb Bach als Vorstellungsschreiben für die Mizler-Gesellschaft in Leipzig, deren Mitglied er 1747 wurde. Diese beiden Werke zeigen, wie wichtig ihm die Kanonform war und wie sehr er seine Fähigkeit, mit ihr zu jonglieren, schätzte, so sehr, dass er sie als seine Visitenkarte und sogar sie als für einen Monarchen würdiges Geschenk betrachtete. Sogar im *Büchlein für Anna Magdalena* wählte er einen Kanon (Kanon, BWV Anh.120), als Teil dieses obersten Liebesbeweises.

Neben den früheren Musikstücken werden seine kurzen Kanons BWV 1072-86, im Allgemeinen, als pädagogisches Material für seine Kinder und Schüler oder als Gelegenheitsstücke (BWV 1073) oder umgekehrt als heilig (Kanontriplex BWV 1076) betrachtet und eingestuft [9]. in Abbildung 1 sehen wir den ersten Kanon.

Auch in der Kunst der Fuge WV 1080 zeigte Bach deutlich vierstimmige Kanons und komplexe Strukturen ("*canon alla duodecima in contrappunto alla quinta*", "due canoni per

Abbildung 1: Man kann hier beobachten, dass die Melodielinie oszilliert, wie eine Welle, eine Sinusfunktion, und dass es vier Stimmen gibt, die in die Taktlinien passen, und vier Stimmen (die Zwischenstimmen), die sie überlappen und einen komplexeren rhythmischen Effekt erzeugen. Das gleiche Element wiederholt sich unendlich. Eine neunte Stimme wäre natürlich identisch mit der ersten.

augmentationem in contrario motu"), sie gelten nicht als bloße Übungen, sondern als eigenständige Musikstücke.

Die Entdeckung der 14 Kanons BWV 1087, einer einzigen Seite (vgl. Abb. 2), die erst 1974 am Ende von Bachs persönlicher Abschrift der Goldberg-Variationen BWV 988 gefunden wurde, offenbarte der Welt, wie raffiniert und komplex die Kanonstruktur in seinem Kopf sein konnte: horizontale und vertikale Symmetrievarianten, Erforschung von Zeitverdoppelungen und Zeithalbierungen, zusätzlich zu den für Kanons typischen Zeitverschiebungen. Diese Seite gilt für die Kanons als Leitfaden, sie wurde schon ausführlich erläutert, diskutiert und illustriert vgl. [2], [3], [4], [5].

Abbildung 2: BWV 1087 Holograpisches Manuscript, n.d.(ca.1741-46)
https://imslp.org/wiki/File:PMLP326356-N55005962_(BWV_1087).pdf

Als Folge dieser Entdeckung erschienen sogar einige Artikel (wie z. B. [6a], [7], [8]) über die mathematischen Transformationen, die beschrieben, wie Bach Kanons komponierte. Diese Artikel aber können bestenfalls dazu dienen, neue Werkzeuge für Kompositionshilfssoftware zu entwickeln, und bringen keine interessanten musikalischen oder musikwissenschaftlichen Erkenntnisse.

1867 Friedrich August Helfer, mit seinem *Canon für 2 Clav. u. Pedal, Bach über Bach* (in: Album für die Orgel zu J. G. Töpfers goldner Amts-Jubelfeier am 4. Juni 1867. - Weimar: T. F. A. Kühn, 1867, S. 54-55), untersuchte einen versteckten Kanon in einem Orgelstück.

Alle diese Veröffentlichungen haben nicht dazu beigetragen, J.S. Bachs Fähigkeit zu verstehen, mehrstimmige Kanons in seinen Meisterwerken zu verstecken.

Im 10. Stück des Musikalischen Opfers BWV 1079 (Canon a 4 quaerendo invenietis) beweist Bach seine Begabung, komplexe Kanons zu komponieren. Jedoch wurde diese Begabung zu seinen Lebzeiten nie ausreichend gewürdigt: Der kriegerische König von Preußen war bei seinem Besuch nicht sehr beeindruckt, vielleicht hatte man ihm einen Kanonexperten versprochen, dabei hatte er vielleicht eher einen Experten für seine geliebten Kriegskanonen erwartet!

Schlimmer noch, J.S. Bachs theoretische Kanonslehren, die er in den oben erwähnten Vorlesungen, Büchlein und Zusammenfassungen für seine geliebten Kinder und seine Frau hinterlassen hat, scheinen in seinen Hauptwerken nicht in vollem Umfang angewandt worden zu sein. Seine Wertschätzung der Kanons als die höchste Form der Schöpfung wurde nie vollständig verstanden. Das 1746 von Elias Gottlob Haussmann angefertigte Porträt von J.S. Bach (das einzige uns erhaltene Porträt) stellt den 13. Kanon in den Vordergrund. So zeigt uns dieser Sachverhalt Bachs wichtigstes Vermächtnis: ein musikalisches Testament!

Bisher habe ich nur die expliziten Kanons erwähnt, die in seinen verschiedenen Werken sichtbar und Musikwissenschaftlern und vielen Musikern sehr vertraut sind.

Diese Kanons sind mehr oder weniger leicht zu hören oder zu erkennen, jedenfalls heute, dank der pädagogischen Videos [10].

Hier geht es dagegen um die immanenten, unvermuteten, unbekannten und verborgenen Kanons in vielen Werken. Diese Kanons sind geheim geblieben; ich möchte sie nach drei Jahrhunderten schwer zu erklärender und unverzeihlicher Unaufmerksamkeit ans Licht bringen.

2 Die Entdeckung der verborgenen Kanons: Ein liebenswertes Abenteuer

2.1 Ein paar Worte zu den Suiten von J.S. Bach

Die Tanzsuite ist eine musikalische Form, die einen doppelten französischen Einfluss auf J.S. Bach zeigt. Zum einen, am offensichtlichsten, ist die Faszination, die er (und ganz allgemein die kleinen deutschsprachigen Höfe) für den großen Hof des Sonnenkönigs Ludwig XIV. empfand, wo der Tanz die absolute Herrschaft des Königs über die Adligen und Damen des Hofes physisch darstellte. Zum anderen, ein subtilerer philosophischer Einfluss (von Descartes, über dem komplexeren Spinoza, bis zu Leibniz), der das Denken und den Glauben im deutschen Raum zur Zeit Bachs zweifellos beherrschte: Das Bedürfnis nach universeller Harmonie, der Sinn eines strukturierten Universums voller Ordnung und Schönheit, das die Vollkommenheit seines göttlichen Schöpfers widerspiegelt. In den Gegenden wurde die Ordnung von der sittenstrengen Kirche Luthers und Calvins (besonders streng nach der schrecklichen Zeit des Martyriums der Täufer) geschätzt und gefürchtet.

Fasziniert und inspiriert wurde Bach in seinen Kompositionen und Improvisationen aber sicherlich auch von der ganz anderen, inkohärenten, lockeren Welt der italienischen katholischen Kirche. Diese musikalische Welt hatte Seiten voller Fantasie und Improvisation, virtuoser Verzierungen und Spezialeffekte, wie in den Concerti Grossi.

Die Suite der Barocktänze beginnt mit einer Ouvertüre, gefolgt von einer Abfolge von Tänzen unterschiedlicher Intensität und Geschwindigkeit, um eine zu große Anstrengung zu vermeiden. Typischerweise finden wir die Allemande, die Courante, die Sarabande und die Gigue. Nach dem 17. Jahrhundert wurden weitere Tänze integriert und aufgenommen, wie Menuett, Bourrée, Gavotte, Passepied, Rigaudon ...

Was die Suiten für Cello betrifft, war Marin Marais (1656-1728) ein berühmter Vorläufer und Bezugspunkt mit seinen *Pièces de viole*, die sicherlich Bachs Werk beeinflussten: Das erste Buch dieser Pièces (1686) war in der Tat eine sehr vollständige Suite (Prélude - Fantaisie - Allemande - Double - Courante - Double - Sarabande - Gigue - Double) und erklärt Bachs Verwendung der Bezeichnungen "Double" und "Phantasie" in seinen Kompositionen. Die *Suitte d'un Goût Étranger* von Marin Marais besteht aus nicht weniger als 33 Tänzen!

Bach fügte den Cello-Suiten immer ein paar "galante Tänze" hinzu, verdoppelte ein anderes Stück wie die Courante, fügte ein Paar Zwillingsstücke ein (die "Doubles" genannt wurden), einen exotischen Tanz wie die Siciliana, oder ließ sogar den Namen einiger Stücke der Partiten und Sonaten für Violine weg, so dass nur die Angabe des Tempos/Charakters blieb (Presto, Adagio, Largo, Allegro etc....).

J.S. Bach schlug, wie Marin Marais, seine Suiten für Soloinstrumente als geniale Form der Unterhaltung für einen kleinen Hof vor, im idealen Stil des opulenten Versailles, aber mit den bescheidenen Kosten eines einzigen Musikers für eine ganze Tanzsitzung, wie an den Höfen der Renaissance mit ihren wandernden Spielleuten. Unüberhörbar bei Bach sind die Präludien, die oft durch die Komplexität einer Fuge bereichert werden, wegen ihres musikalischen Interesses und ihrer doppelten Funktion als Vorbereitung für Tänze und als

Unterhaltung für eine gesellige Zusammenkunft von Menschen, die sich unterhalten, wie die moderne "Piano Bar". Neben dem formalen Aspekt dieser Tänze zeigt Bachs kostbares Werk deutlich seine solide Struktur und präsentiert Melodien, die in die Seele des Zuhörers eindringen und die Schönheit des Universums in Klang umsetzen.

Unter Musikwissenschaftlern gibt es verschiedene Diskussionen über den Stil der Tänze, ob sie eher italienisch oder französisch sind, aber das Wichtigste ist die allgemeine und ideale Absicht der Suiten: Sogar die "englischen Suiten" wurden mit der Absicht und in der Hoffnung komponiert und angeboten, am englischen Hof geschätzt zu werden, aber immer mit dem Ziel, die Atmosphäre und den Glanz des französischen Hofes wiederzugeben.

Man kann auch unterscheiden zwischen den Suiten für Cembalo, ein mehrstimmiges Instrument, die vor der Köthener Zeit komponiert wurden, und den Suiten für Cello/Violine/Flöte solo, die eine kompositorische Herausforderung darstellten (von Marin Marais initiiert): Sie mussten eine Tanzsitzung mit nur einem Melodieinstrument beleben, mit dem zusätzlichen Problem, den Rhythmus zu vermitteln, wie es in der Straßenmusik, in Tavernen oder auf Schiffen gebräuchlich war, aber nicht an Fürstenhöfen. Man kann spekulieren, dass diese Suiten als "Reisegarnitur" für den Wanderer Fürst Leopold von Köthen entstanden sein könnten, um die Anzahl und die Kosten der Musiker auf Reisen zu minimieren.

Eine letzte Bemerkung: Der meditative und wandernde Charakter vieler Stücke für Violine und Cello, den wir heute vor Augen haben, ist ein deformierendes Erbe der spätromantischen Interpretationen vergangener Jahrhunderte, die diese Suiten als reine Salonmusik, die nichts mit Tänzen zu tun hat, oder als reine technische Übungen (!) betrachteten. In den letzten Jahrzehnten haben mehrere Interpreten gezeigt, wie die Tänze der Suiten für

Cello vollständig als Tänze gespielt werden können, mit ihrem ursprünglichen rhythmischen Charakter. Die Suiten für Cembalo haben unter dieser romantischen Fehlinterpretation weniger gelitten.

2.2 Enthüllung der Geheimnisse der 2. Cello Suite

2.2.1 Das Präludium der 2. Suite

1984 spielte ich als Gymnasiast zufällig die Suiten für Cello Solo in einem Raum mit Holzverkleidung (eine kleine Kapelle in den französischen Alpen, ziemlich schallend und hallig) und war von einem seltsamen Klangeffekt beeindruckt: Während des Spiels hatte ich den Eindruck, dass ich mich selbst begleitete. Ich versprach mir, dem nachzugehen.
Im Sommer 1991 hörte ich beim Spielen des Prélude aus der 2. Suite genau hin und sang den Anfang dieses melodischen Stücks und stellte fest, dass es im Kanon funktioniert. Nach einer kurzen schriftlichen Analyse erkannte ich, dass das gesamte Prélude als Kanon funktioniert. Bei diesem Stück habe ich die Schlussakkorde (schlecht) so entwickelt, dass die Melodie im Kanon weiterläuft. Zuletzt habe ich das Stück als Duett gedruckt, das mit zwei Celli oder mit Violine (Oktave) und Cello gespielt werden kann.

Ein paar Jahre später, testete ich es mit einem Freund zusammen und stellte fest, dass einige Teile nicht gut funktionierten, also versprach ich mir, sie so schnell wie möglich zu beheben.
Im Jahr 2019 (!), nahm ich das Stück schließlich auf einem Computer mit neuer Basissoftware wieder auf und stellte fest, dass es tatsächlich einige problematische Teile gab.

Es dauerte eine Weile, bis ich eine Lösung für den Kanon gefunden hatte, da dies eine komplette Umgestaltung der Melodie erforderte. Außerdem begann ich mich zu fragen, warum Bach diese Takte nicht wie den Rest des Stücks im Kanon komponiert hatte. Da ich keine Antwort fand, nahm ich meine Analyse des Stücks wieder auf und sah, dass es Platz für eine dritte Stimme im Kanon gab: Ich versuchte es sofort und es funktionierte! Ich werde später erklären, warum ich gerade in eine viel komplexere Welt eingetreten war: Es kostete nun viel mehr Zeit und Mühe, eine Lösung für die problematischen Takte zu finden, und sogar die Entwicklung der Schlussakkorde musste überarbeitet werden. Außerdem war jede Lösung, die ich gefunden habe (es gibt nicht nur eine Lösung für dieses Problem), im Vergleich zum Rest von Bachs Original musikalisch unbefriedigend. Schließlich war es für den dreistimmigen Kanon auch notwendig, einige sporadische Noten im Rest des Stücks zu korrigieren, was dessen melodische Linearität ziemlich zerstörte. Auch in jüngerer Zeit, im Jahr 2023, habe ich versucht, bessere Lösungen zu finden (vor allem für die Entwicklung der Schlussakkorde), aber die Reihe der

Abbildung 3: 2. Cello Suite, 2 stimmiger Kanon

problematischen Takte besteht immer noch: Sie bleiben eine gute Übung, wenn Sie sich selbst daran versuchen wollen!

Meine Erklärung, warum dieser Teil des Originalstücks (identisch in Anna Magdalenas und Kellners Version) nicht als Kanon funktionierte, war, dass J.S. Bach die Suite kurz nach dem plötzlichen Tod seiner Frau komponiert hatte und an den Abschnitten und am Ende des Stücks eine "Lücke" mit einigen akkordischen Angaben gelassen hatte, die "später vervollständigt" werden sollten. Wahrscheinlich fand er nie die Kraft, dieses Stück zu vollenden, weil er es schmerzlich mit Trauer verband, und das Stück wurde von der launischen und eleganten Anna Magdalena Wilcke ergänzt und korrigiert. Eine andere mögliche Version ist, dass niemand verstand, warum er so lange brauchte, um ein einfaches Stück für Solocello zu vollenden, und dass er es in aller Eile zwischen Engagements fertigstellen musste, um es zu verkaufen, aber das glaube ich nicht, denn die Suiten wurden zuerst seinem Schüler Kellner gegeben und erst viele Jahre später veröffentlicht. Vielleicht sollte er sie Kellner oder einem anderen Cellisten anlässlich eines Hofballs schenken, auf jeden Fall hatte sich die wahrscheinliche ursprüngliche Absicht, ein Geschenk für Fürst Leopold zu sein, der Viola da Gamba spielte, in Luft aufgelöst, denn der Fürst war kein großer Musiker und die Suiten waren nicht sehr leicht zu spielen, so dass es keine Eile gab, das "Geschenkpaket" zu vervollständigen.

2.2.2   Die unentwickelten Schlussakkorde

Nach dieser Entdeckung ist der alte Streit zwischen Cellisten darüber, ob die Schlussakkorde des Prélude zur 2. Suite als Grundlage für eine Improvisation genutzt werden sollten oder nicht, meiner Meinung nach beigelegt: Angesichts des kurzen Zeitintervalls zwischen den verschiedenen Stimmen könnte man sogar eine verkürzte Version der Akkorde akzeptieren, wie in Abbildung 5, um Überschneidungen zu vermeiden, aber ich bin davon überzeugt, dass sie für eine Improvisation genutzt werden sollten, um den Dreierkanon auf melodische und diskursive Weise zu vervollständigen, wie im Beispiel in Abbildung 6.

Abbild 4: original Schlussakkorde

Abbild 5: kurze Akkorden laut einem 3 stimmingen Kanon

Abbild 6: laut einem 3 stimmigen Kanon entwickelte Akkorden

2.2.3 Enthüllung des Rests der zweiten Solo-Cello-Suite

Zu diesem Zeitpunkt dachte ich, dass die Entdeckung eines dreistimmigen Kanons, der in einem so schönen und langen Stück wie dem Prélude versteckt ist, ein bemerkenswertes Unikat in der Musikgeschichte sei, aber nur zum Spaß versuchte ich, die Analyse auf das zweite Stück der Suite, die Allemande, auszudehnen: Unglaublicherweise war auch sie ein doppelter Kanon, woraufhin ich die Schätze aller Tänze, einen nach dem anderen, die Courante, die Sarabande, die beiden Menuette und die Gigue, enthüllte. Ich musste die Partitur Note für Note abschreiben, dabei nutzte ich die wenige Zeit, die ich Ende 2021 an den Wochenenden hatte. Glücklicherweise gab es bei den Tänzen keine Probleme wie beim Prélude, nur ein paar falsche Noten, die "korrigiert" werden mussten, aber bei jedem entdeckten Dreifach-Kanon war die Freude und das Vergnügen groß, etwas Neues zu hören, denn unglaublich, selbst wenn man das Stück auswendig kennt und zusammensetzt, kann man sich vorher nicht vorstellen, wie der Gegenkanon klingt, und das bei einer ganzen Suite von Tänzen: Ich hatte jahrelang auf der Schatzkiste gesessen, ohne es zu merken! Schließlich habe ich die Noten auf einigen Websites (IMSLP und AIMA music) veröffentlicht und die Entdeckung in einem Webinar vorgestellt.

2.3 *Die Geheimnisse der anderen fünf Cellosuiten*

In den folgenden Monaten des Jahres 2022 dehnte ich die Suche auf die anderen Suiten für Cello aus und entdeckte die gleiche verborgene Struktur des dreistimmigen Kanons, sogar im unvermuteten Präludium und der Fuge der fünften Suite, die die doppelte Struktur von Gegenkanon und Fuge aufweist: ein absolutes Meisterwerk! Das letzte Stück der letzten Suite, eine Gigue, funktioniert sogar als 10-stimmiger Kanon! Ich habe es für das Bläserensemble angepasst und etwas vereinfacht (um die Klangfarben der einzelnen Stimmen besser unterscheiden zu können).

Interessanterweise passen einige Passagen oder einzelne Noten nicht in den dreistimmigen Kanon, z. B. im Präludium der ersten Suite: Vielleicht hat Bach ein "Loch" gelassen, das später vervollständigt werden soll, oder ein Unfall hat die Partitur verwischt (Wasser auf Tinte, nagende Maus?) und jemand (Anna Magdalena?) hat eine vernünftige Melodie gefunden, um sie zu vervollständigen.

Die Art und Weise, wie der Kanon funktioniert, ist sehr vielfältig, und das machte diese Suche zu einer Reise voller Überraschungen, bei der es sich lohnt, die versteckten Effekte zu hören. Außerdem stellte ich fest, dass es in jeder Suite ein einziges Stück gab, das sogar als 7-stimmiger Kanon funktionierte (wenn man parallele 4. und 5. toleriert), ohne dass die Klarheit der Struktur sofort verloren ging, ein anderes Stück für jede der sechs Suiten, das zusammen mit den anderen Ausnahmen eine 'siebte Suite für 7 Celli' bildete.

Ein Forscher [6b] schlug vor, alle Cellosuiten Bachs Frau zuzuschreiben, aber ich würde sagen, dass ich nach dieser Untersuchung (insbesondere für die folgenden Abschnitte) sagen kann, dass das innere Hören der Kanons in drei (oder mehr) Stimmen wie eine Signatur von J.S. Bach ist, die niemand nachahmen kann. Ich werde, im zweiten Teil des Büchleins, erklären warum.

In den Anhängen habe ich den Link zu den Kanons der Suiten für Cello (mit dem Beginn jedes Stücks und dem Intervall zwischen den Stimmen) angegeben und ich habe einige Hörproben auf YouTube gestellt, um einen Vorgeschmack auf die Kanons zu geben.

2.4 Die Entdeckung der Suiten für andere Soloinstrumente

Nach der Analyse von 6x7 = 42 Stücken in den Suiten für Violoncello wurde mir klar, dass J.S. Bach ein "serieller Kanonist" war: Er hatte eine natürliche und spontane Art, Melodien zu hören und zu komponieren, die Kanons verbargen, wie eine Berufskrankheit (es gab so viele davon!), aus einem mysteriösen Grund, den ich klären musste.

Um dies zu überprüfen, musste ich weitere Stücke untersuchen. Mit der These von den "Reisepaketen" für Fürst Leopold im Hinterkopf habe ich im ersten Quartal 2022 die Analyse auf die anderen von Bach an Leopolds Hof komponierten Werke für melodische Soloinstrumente ausgedehnt: die Suiten für Violine und die für Querflöte.

Denken Sie daran, dass ich mit "Analyse eines Stücks" eigentlich das geduldige Kopieren der Partitur Note für Note auf dem Computer meine, ähnlich wie Bach selbst es auf dem Papier tat, als er ein Junge war und die Meisterwerke seiner Zeitgenossen entdeckte, nur ohne den Stress, keine Fehler zu machen, keine Tintenflecken zu machen, keine Federn zu zerbrechen und kein Papier zu verschwenden und dafür bestraft zu werden! Der zweite Schritt ist einfacher als die vorherige Arbeit: Ein einfaches Kopieren und Einfügen des ersten Eintrags in anderen Stimmen, dabei wird es nach dem richtigen Zeitversatz gesucht, um eine Übereinstimmung von mindestens 80 % zu erreichen, die ansprechend und formal sinnvoll ist. In der heutigen Zeit gibt es bequemere Möglichkeiten, diese Arbeit zu erledigen (leider ist mir das erst später eingefallen!): Suchen Sie einfach eine bereits transkribierte Datei auf Websites wie Musescore, oder suchen Sie eine Datei im Midi-Format und importieren Sie sie in ein Textverarbeitungsprogramm für Musik, Diskettenspaß. Das geht viel schneller, aber man lernt viel weniger, und vor allem wenn man von Audiodateien ausgeht, kann die Transkription im Vergleich zum Original rhythmisch sehr falsch sein, und die Partitur ist völlig falsch. Außerdem verpasst man das Vergnügen, die Originalpartituren zu lesen, die von Bach und seiner Familie/Firma handgeschrieben wurden, mit den Kommentarzeichen, den eleganten Linien, die bereits die Interpretation andeuten: Musik für die Augen, und das ganze Vergnügen, Fehler oder Diskrepanzen zwischen verschiedenen Versionen zu finden, kurz gesagt, der ganze Geschmack der Geschichte fehlt!

Da in den Violinsuiten mehr Noten zu kopieren sind, als in den Cellosuiten, konzentrierte ich mich direkt auf die Suche nach den "besonderen Stücken" der sechs Sonaten und Partiten (BWV 1001-1006), die als siebenstimmige Kanons fungierten, in der

Hoffnung, dass, wie in den Cellosuiten, jede Suite ein verschiedenes Stück verstecken würde.

Ich begann mit meinen Lieblingsstücken und sah, dass sie gut funktionierten, also hörte ich dort auf und beschränkte mich auf sieben Stücke, die ich wiederum die 'versteckte siebte Suite für Violine solo' nannte. Für meine musikwissenschaftlichen Freunde, die die Arbeit fortsetzen wollen, stehen die anderen Violinstücke zur Verfügung, damit sie ihre Gegenstücke enthüllen und sie nach dreihundert Jahren anhören können: Ich versichere Ihnen, dass sie es wert sind und die Zeit gut investiert ist!

Damit blieb nur noch die Partita BWV 1013 für Querflöte übrig: Allemande, Courante, Sarabande, Bourrée und Anglaise enthüllten ihre verborgenen Kanons für vier Stimmen. Um diese unglückliche, scheinbar unvollendete Suite zu "vervollständigen", habe ich einen Blick auf andere berühmte Stücke von Bach für Soloflöte oder begleitete Flöte geworfen: Es fehlte ein Präludium, das mit BWV 846 identifiziert wurde, und ich fügte die Badinerie BWV 1067 als letztes Stück hinzu, was ihre verborgenen Kanons enthüllte. Wahrscheinlich hatte Bach das Material für Flöte solo aus der kompletten Suite wiederverwendet, um aufwändigere und erfolgreichere Werke zu schaffen. Ich muss zugeben, dass das klangliche und musikalische Ergebnis der Suite für Flöte mit mehrstimmigen Kanons viel weniger befriedigend und überzeugend ist als dasjenige der Suiten für Violine oder Cello. Dies mag erklären, warum Bach sich frei fühlte, die Suite zu zerstückeln und nur ihre Überreste in BWV 1013 zu belassen. Um die Flötensuite weiter zu bereichern, habe ich kürzlich die Gigue aus der Lautensuite BWV 997, die als fünfstimmiger Kanon funktioniert, und das berühmte Siciliano aus der Sonate BWV 1031, das als siebenstimmiger Kanon funktioniert, analysiert.

Zu diesem Zeitpunkt hatte ich die Suiten für Melodieinstrumente abgeschlossen, mit einer einzigen Stimme, die vielleicht eine immanente Begleitung benötigt. Aber beim Anhören der Suiten für Tasteninstrumente, der Französischen Suiten (BWV 812-817) und der Englischen Suiten (BWV 806-811), fiel mir auf, dass die Notendichte angesichts der zehn zur Verfügung stehenden Finger nicht sehr hoch war: obwohl perfekt, waren sie eher spärlich. Also analysierte ich in den Sommerferien 2022 alle Anfänge aller Stücke der Suiten und fand die versteckte Struktur des dreistimmigen Kanons: alle diese Suiten können von drei Cembali oder Klavieren gespielt werden. Auch hier habe ich die Französischen Suiten mit den fehlenden Präludien "ergänzt", die ich aus den von Bach vorbereiteten "freien" Präludien entnommen und tonal angeglichen habe (BWV 935, BWV 934, BWV 925, BWV 876, BWV 816, BWV 937). Die Analyse dieser Suiten für Cembalo war für mich sehr aufschlussreich, denn sie wurden nicht in der Köthener Zeit für Fürst Leopold geschrieben, sondern früher. Folglich war meine Hypothese der "Reisesuite für Leopold" nicht unbedingt richtig! Auf jeden Fall bleibt festzuhalten, dass Partituren für einen einzelnen Musiker, die eine Ballgesellschaft beleben können, kommerziell eine großartige Idee waren, und dass diejenigen für Cembalo von Bach selbst für mögliche Reisen verwendet werden konnten. Ich denke, dass die ersten Suiten, die komponiert wurden, die französischen waren, aus den im Abschnitt über die Einflüsse genannten Gründen, ohne die Präludien, mit der Idee, jedes Mal ein anderes zu wählen oder zu improvisieren, bevor man die Tänze spielt, weshalb wir viele separate und lose Präludien finden, in vielen Tönen und Stimmungen, für jede Gelegenheit.

2.5 Die Konsequenzen für das Spielen der Bachschen Suiten

Nach diesen Entdeckungen kann ein Musiker meiner Meinung nach die Suiten in den üblichen Konzertsälen weiterhin allein spielen, da Bach seine mehrstimmigen Kanons nicht explizit gemacht hat. Aber jetzt kann man sie auch in einer Gruppe spielen, oder mit Hilfe eines Tonsystems, das künstliche Echos hinzufügt, oder indem man sich in echoreiche Umgebungen begibt und die Spielzeit an den Saal anpasst (wie es mir 1984 passiert ist), um ein größeres Publikum die Wunder der mehrstimmigen Kanons entdecken zu lassen. Was die Interpretation der Suiten angeht, so können die Musiker weiterhin ihre romantisierenden und extrem manieristischen Versionen machen, aber sie sollten jetzt wissen, dass Bach sie mit Sicherheit nicht so gehört hat. Das Vorhandensein von zwei zusätzlichen Stimmen ist völlig unvereinbar mit plötzlichen Tempowechseln und übermäßigem Atmen zwischen zwei Phrasen, die von den Romantikern missbraucht werden. Seien Sie sicher, dass die Vermeidung von Pausen und die Annahme eines gleichmäßigen Tempos oder kleiner progressiver Variationen (Beschleunigungen und Verlangsamungen) der ursprünglichen Absicht und dem Vorhandensein des immanenten Kanons besser entsprechen.

Abschließend möchte ich betonen, dass das Spielen der Suiten im Kanon mit mehreren Instrumenten eine ausgezeichnete musikalische Übung ist, denn es erfordert eine genaue Kontrolle des Tempos, die wir beim alleinigen Spielen nicht gewohnt sind, und eine perfekte Kontrolle der Klangintensität der verschiedenen Stimmen, da die Melodien auch zur Begleitung werden: Mein Vorschlag ist, immer die erste Stimme lauter zu spielen und die anderen allmählich schwächer werden zu lassen, wie es bei natürlichen Echos geschieht.

2.6 *Exzentrischer Exkurs über die Numerologie*

Hier muss ich ein paar Worte über die Numerologie in Bachs Suiten sagen. Es ist ein frivoles Thema, aber eines, welches es verdient, näher untersucht zu werden. Zu J.S. Bachs Zeiten war die Numerologie ein wichtiges und allgegenwärtiges Wissen, das jeder mehr oder weniger, gewollt oder ungewollt, nutzte, um seine geistigen Gewohnheiten und Überzeugungen, wie Aberglauben, auf der Grundlage persönlicher Erfahrungen oder kollektiver Regeln und Konventionen zu konstruieren. Schaut man sich die vollständige Liste der von J.S. Bach komponierten Suiten an (z.B. unter https://en.wikipedia.org/wiki/Suite_(Bach) oder im offiziellen Leipziger Archiv), so stellt man sofort fest, dass sie aus mehreren vollständigen Gruppen von sechs Suiten besteht: eine Gruppe für Cello (BWV 1007-1012), eine für Violine (BWV 1001-1006), vier für Cembalo (BWV 806-811, BWV 812-817, BWV 825-830, BWV 818-824). In jeder Suite gibt es in der Regel sechs Tänze. Sie sehen also, dass man bei sechs Sätzen die "satanische Zahl" 666 erhalten würde, was für eine Musik, die als höchster religiöser Ausdruck gilt, absolut inakzeptabel ist (vgl. [9b]). Glücklicherweise gibt es noch einige weitere Suiten: die Suiten und Ouvertüren für Cembalo (BWV 831, BWV 832-845) oder Laute (BWV 995-998) oder Orchester (BWV 1066-1069-1070?), ganz zu schweigen von den "freien" Sätzen (meist Präludien). Als weiteres Dementi möchte ich hinzufügen, dass die Einteilung in Gruppen erst nach Bachs Tod erfolgte, so dass es keinen Grund gibt, satanische Absichten seitens Bachs zu vermuten, und Sie können diesen Absatz genauso gut vergessen.

Aber bei diesem numerologischen Thema müssen wir bedenken, dass J.S. Bach der siebte Sohn von sieben Kindern einer großartigen Familie war, die sieben Jahre lang ein musikalisches Paradies um ihn herum aufbaute, bevor sie zusammenbrach. Außerdem erhielt er seine musikalische Ausbildung in der Michaeliskirche in Ohrdruf und der Michaelschule in Lüneburg. Nun ist St. Michael der Engel, der die erste der sieben Posaunen der Apokalypse bläst. Daraus folgt, dass Bach ein positives Verhältnis zur Zahl Sieben gehabt haben muss, ganz abgesehen davon, dass die Zahl Sieben in der westlichen Kultur im Allgemeinen als Glückszahl gilt, die mit dem siebten Tag, dem Tag der Ruhe, in Verbindung gebracht wird und somit für die

Vollendung des Schöpfungszyklus (in der Bibel) und die Heilige Woche der von Bach mehrfach vertonten christlichen Passion steht, während die Zahl Sechs für eine unvollständige und inakzeptable Schöpfung steht. Dies mag erklären, warum Bach in den Cellosuiten und vielen anderen das Präludium als siebten Satz einfügte (und später komponierte), der die sechs Tänze krönt, wobei er dem Beispiel von Marin Marais folgte (der die Zahl der Tänze weniger genau angab). Zu den Französischen Suiten gehören auch die begleitenden Präludien und Fugen, einschließlich derjenigen aus dem Wohltemperierten Klavier. Wie bereits erwähnt, war das Präludium nicht nur eine Komposition, die eine bestimmte Atmosphäre und einen bestimmten Stil für die spielerische Zeit der Tänze vorbereitete, sondern auch eine virtuosere und phantasievollere Form der Unterhaltung, die zu hören war. Auf jeden Fall habe ich die "versteckte siebte Suite" für Cello und die für Violine in dieser numerologischen Logik der symbolischen Vervollständigung und der Notwendigkeit, die sechs sechsteiligen Suiten zu vermeiden, vorgeschlagen. Was die vier Suiten für Cembalo betrifft, so denke ich, dass es nicht notwendig ist, in einigen Stücken nach weiteren komplexen Merkmalen zu suchen, um die siebte Suite zu fabrizieren, da es bereits viele unechte Suiten außerhalb der etablierten Gruppierungen gibt.

2.7 *Ausweitung der Analyse auf andere Meisterwerke*

Ausgehend von der Liste der Suiten und den obigen Beobachtungen sind noch viele andere mehrstimmige Kanons verborgen, die von skeptischen Lesern entdeckt werden können, sowohl in den Partiten und Sonaten als auch in den Suiten für Cembalo oder für Laute: Probieren Sie es aus, um es zu glauben. Ich habe sie für den Ruhestand aufgehoben! Um zu verstehen, ob mehrstimmige versteckte Kanons eine systematische Konstante bei J.S. Bach sind, die nicht auf die

Suiten beschränkt ist, habe ich mich in die Analyse einiger Konzerte gestürzt. Ich entdeckte, dass:

1) Im Violinkonzert BWV 1041 verbirgt die Soloviolinstimme einen dreistimmigen Kanon, d. h. sie kann mit drei Solisten gespielt werden!

2) im Konzert für zwei Violinen BWV 1043 verbergen die beiden Solo-Violinen einen vierstimmigen Kanon, d.h. das Stück kann mit acht Solisten gespielt werden!

3) Im Konzert für Oboe und Violine BWV 1060R verbirgt jede der beiden Solostimmen einen vierstimmigen Kanon, d. h. das Stück kann mit 8 Solisten, 4 Violinen und 4 Oboen, gespielt werden! Darüber hinaus könnten die vier Streicher des Orchesters im ersten Satz auch als vierstimmiger Kanon fungieren, so dass vier Orchester das Stück gleichzeitig spielen könnten...

4) im Allegro des 5. Brandenburgischen Konzerts sind die Solostimmen der Flöte und der Violine mit einem vierstimmigen Kanon kompatibel, d.h. das Stück kann mit nur 4 Violinen und 4 Flöten gespielt werden.

5) Ich habe in den anderen Sätzen des 5. Brandenburgischen Konzerts keine funktionierenden versteckten Kanons finden können, was bedeutet, dass

   a. vielleicht hat J.S. Bach die versteckten Kanons nicht verwendet, wenn er keine Zeit oder Lust dazu hatte, oder er hat die Aufgabe, die Stücke zu vollenden, an seine Frau oder Kinder/Töchter delegiert, ohne die versteckten Kanons zu benötigen.

   b. In jedem Fall impliziert die kontrapunktische Komposition allein nicht die Möglichkeit, mehrstimmige versteckte Kanons zu finden!

Alle Partituren, die aus diesen Recherchen hervorgegangen sind, sind auf der IMSLP (siehe die Rubriken "Arrangements" und "Sonstiges") und AIMAmusic (https://aimamusic.it/nuova-musica/) frei verfügbar.

2.8 Kontrapunktische Einwände

Einige Musiker haben mir gesagt, dass das Auffinden von Kanons in einer kontrapunktischen Komposition eine Selbstverständlichkeit ist. Diese Beobachtung gilt (nicht immer) für zweistimmige Kanons oder für einfache Melodien mit einem oszillierenden Muster, das in regelmäßigen Zyklen wiederholt wird, wie das Beispiel des Kanons BWV 1072 von Bach, aber sie wird völlig falsch, wenn es um dreistimmige Kanons und komplexe Melodien wie die der Suiten geht. Es genügt, wenn sich bestimmte Takte in einer Weise verändern, die mit den vorangegangenen Takten unvereinbar ist, wie z. B. die problematischen Takte der zweiten Cellosuite oder die der anderen Sätze der fünften. Wenn Sie davon nicht überzeugt sind, versuchen Sie, einen dreistimmigen Kanon zu komponieren, und Sie werden es verstehen, oder suchen Sie nach versteckten Kanons in kontrapunktischen Werken anderer Autoren! Im folgenden Kapitel werden die Feinheiten von Bachs mehrstimmigen Kanons näher erläutert, und es handelt sich nicht um die bekannten Kanons, die auf dem Leitfaden/Text BWV 1087 basieren.

3   Die Schwierigkeit, mehrstimmige Kanons zu komponieren

3.1 Was ist ein Kanon?

Der Kanon ist im musikalischen Sinne eine interessante Art, eine Melodie zu begleiten, indem man dieselbe Melodie zeitlich verzögert als zweite Stimme verwendet. Aus symbolischer Sicht stellt der Kanon die verschiedenen Generationen dar, die in verschiedenen Momenten ihrer Existenz nebeneinander existieren, indem sie in zeitlich gestaffelten Momenten geboren werden und sterben, eine nach der anderen. Der Kanon wird oft in unendlichen zyklischen Formen verwendet, wobei die Melodie wieder von vorne beginnt, sobald sie endet, und so dem "panta rei" der alten Griechen, bei dem sich die Geschichte endlos wiederholt, oder der hinduistischen Metempsychose eine klangliche Form gibt.

In der Kompositionspraxis muss sich jedes Element der komponierten Melodie, um als Kanon zu funktionieren, mit dem nächsten Element ebenso überschneiden können wie mit dem vorherigen. Die Länge des "Elements" entspricht der zeitlichen Verzögerung zwischen den Stimmen.

In Volksliedern findet man oft eine vereinfachte Form des Kanons, in der die Elemente der Melodie wiederholt oder abgewechselt werden und mit sich selbst identisch sind, so dass nur zwei miteinander kompatible Elemente benötigt werden.

Die grafische Darstellung dieser "trivialen Kanons" kann erfolgen, indem man für jedes Element der Melodie eine Farbe verwendet und sie auf der laufenden Zeitlinie einzeichnet:

Abbildung 7a: Trivialkanon mit alternierenden Elementen

Abbildung 7b: Trivialkanon mit wiederholten Elementen

Es ist zu beobachten, dass diese trivialen Kanons auch durch Hinzufügen weiterer Stimmen funktionieren, aber im Fall der alternierenden Elemente von Abbildung 7a ist die dritte Stimme identisch mit der ersten, während im Fall der wiederholten Elemente von Abbildung 7b die fünfte Stimme identisch mit der ersten ist. In beiden Fällen sind die sich überlagernden Elemente immer die gleichen, und diese Art von Musik ist schnell langweilig und wird für Kinderlieder verwendet, da Kinder zwanghaft wiederholte Aktivitäten lieben. Dennoch schafft der Effekt der Überlagerung einer skalierten Melodie mit sich selbst eine neue Empfindung, ein Vergnügen sui generis und ein neues Gesamtelement: Es ist das Grundelement der Metamusik (vgl. [11]).

73

Man kann dann "evolutionäre Kanons" finden, in denen sich die aufeinander folgenden Elemente kontinuierlich verändern, ohne sich zu wiederholen. In dieser Form muss jedes Element gleichzeitig mit dem nächsten und dem vorherigen Element, die nicht identisch sind wie im trivialen Kanon, angenehm kompatibel sein. Die grafische Darstellung sieht dann wie folgt aus:

Abbildung 8: Einfacher Evolutivkanon mit wechselnden Elementen

Dieser Kanon ist interessanter und "schwieriger" zu komponieren und vermeidet lästige Wiederholungen.

3.2 Die mehrstimmigen Evolutivkanons

Ab der dritten Stimme ("Doppelkanon") nimmt die Komplexität dramatisch zu, und kaum jemand kann im Voraus hören, wie sich die Überlagerung auswirkt und ob eine Melodie die Anforderungen des dreistimmigen Kanons erfüllen wird: Jedes Element der Melodie muss nämlich *mit den beiden vorangehenden* und *den beiden folgenden* Elementen kompatibel sein:

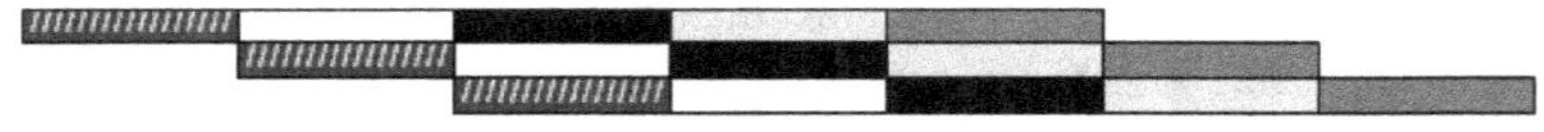

Abbildung 9: Doppelter Evolutivkanon (3 Stimmen)

Je größer die Anzahl der Stimmen ist, die sich in einem sich entwickelnden Kanon überschneiden müssen, desto komplizierter ist das Komponieren der einzelnen Elemente und desto komplizierter ist das Hören: Für n Stimmen muss jedes Element mit 2 x (n-1) Elementen kompatibel sein. Bei 5 Stimmen zum Beispiel muss jedes Element mit 8 Elementen kompatibel sein (4 vor und 4 nach), wie im folgenden Diagramm dargestellt:

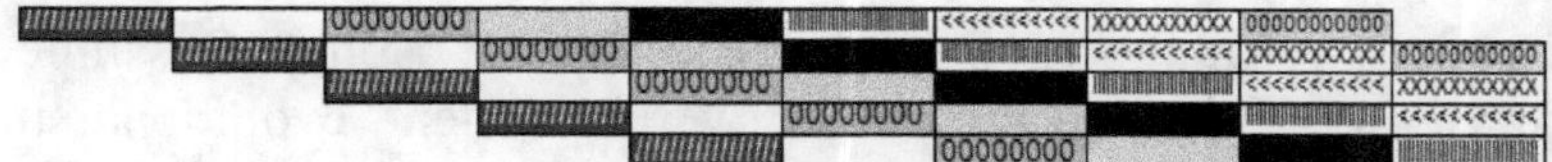

Abbildung 10: 5-stimmiger Evolutivkanon

Jetzt können Sie etwas besser verstehen, warum ich mich mit den fehlenden Takten des Prélude der zweiten Suite herumgeschlagen habe, und Sie können auch verstehen, dass es nicht so einfach ist, den achtstimmigen Kanon in Abbildung 1 zu realisieren, schon gar nicht, wenn er auch noch gefällig sein soll, selbst mit Hilfe eines Computers: Denken Sie an die siebenstimmigen Kanons der Suiten und den zehnstimmigen Kanon der Gigue der letzten Cellosuite. Das Vorhandensein mehrstimmiger versteckter, immanenter Kanons erklärt vollständig die besondere verschlungene Form und den Stil von Bachs Melodien, die man durch den Vergleich mit denen anderer Komponisten beobachten kann und die mich vor dieser Entdeckung immer fasziniert haben.

3.3 Kanonischer Kontext zur Zeit von J.S. Bach

Für ausführlichere Informationen verweise ich auf die Werke von Denis Collins [1] und [4]. Lassen Sie mich nur ein paar Bemerkungen machen. In Anbetracht der bescheidenen Verhältnisse, in denen J.S. Bach während seiner Jahre in Ohrdruf bei seinem großen Bruder, dem Organisten Johann Christoph, lebte, mit wenig (teuren) Noten, die er - vielleicht heimlich - kopieren oder auswendig lernen konnte, scheint es unwahrscheinlich, dass J.S.B. die Ricercari, canone e sonate per 2 violoncelli (1689) von Domenico Gabrielli entdeckt haben könnte, bei denen es sich um evolutionäre Kanons in vereinfachter Form handelt, bei denen sich Abschnitte der Melodie in einer Stimme mit Abschnitten der Begleitung abwechseln, während die Melodie in die zweite Stimme übergeht. Im Gegensatz dazu scheint es sicher zu sein, dass Bach im deutschen Kontext mit dem berühmten Kanon und der Gigue in D-Dur (1680, S.37) von Johann Pachelbel, dem Lehrer seines

Bruders, vertraut war: Dieses Stück hat eine ostinate Basslinie und drei Stimmen in einer vereinfachten evolutionären Kanonform, mit abwechselnden Phrasen und Begleitungen, die Elemente sind lang, bleiben aber in der gleichen Tonart und die Harmonie ist alles in allem arm. Trotz oder vielleicht gerade wegen dieser Einfachheit ist Pachelbels Kanon ein Welterfolg und war zweifellos eine Entdeckung und Referenz für den jungen Bach.

3.4 *Bachs evolutive und modulierende Kanons*

Beide Stücke bleiben jedoch von Anfang bis Ende in der gleichen Tonalität. Im Gegensatz dazu erfordern Bachs evolutionäre Kanons ein höheres Maß an Kompatibilität zwischen benachbarten Elementen, da sie in verschiedenen Tonarten stehen können (modulierende Melodie). Die dreistimmigen evolutionären Kanons sind schon in einer Tonart schwer zu komponieren, erfordern aber das Talent eines Genies, um modulierend zu sein und schöne Melodien zu erhalten. Bach lernte wahrscheinlich auf seinem Lübeck-Abenteuer, bei dem er 400 km zu Fuß zurücklegte, um den berühmten Orgelbauer Dieterich Buxtehude mit seinem Stylus phantasticus und seinen Präludien und Fugen auszuspionieren, wie man die Tonart leicht ändern kann.

Sicherlich sind die Krabbenkanons oder die reflexiven Kanons oder die "per augmentationem oder diminutionem" von BWV 1087 theoretisch noch komplexer, aber andererseits sind sie weniger hörbar und ohne visuelle Unterstützung nicht sehr genießbar. In jedem Fall konzentriert sich diese auf hörbare, modulierende, mehrstimmige, versteckte Kanons.

4 Kommentare zu den beigefügten „Kanonsführer"-Partituren

4.1 *Der kurze Kanonsführer*

In den beiliegenden Partituren finden Sie alle Anfänge der verschiedenen Stücke mit den verschiedenen Verzögerungen zwischen den Kanoneinträgen für die "vollendeten" Französischen und Englischen Suiten und auch für die verschiedenen Konzerte, die ich untersucht habe. Die Tatsache, dass nur die Anfänge der Stücke angegeben werden, spart nicht nur Papier, sondern erlaubt es den Musikern auch, ihre gewohnte Ausgabe weiter zu verwenden und nur die Verzögerung anzuwenden, wenn sie mit anderen Musikern auftreten. Die Suiten für Cello werden stattdessen in ihrer Gesamtheit wiedergegeben, weil ich die schlechte Idee hatte, sie zu "korrigieren", wie ich bereits erklärt habe, was ich nicht noch einmal tun würde, weil die Entdeckung der verborgenen Kanons das Hauptinteresse dieser Arbeit ist und weil die Varianten, die in den Melodien vorgeschlagen wurden, um mit den mehrstimmigen Kanons kompatibler zu sein, immer weniger schön sind als das Original. Selbst in Fällen, in denen Stücke fehlten (Ende der sechsten Suite) oder sichtbar geflickt wurden (zweite Suite für Cello) und eine "konservative Restaurierungsarbeit" für geduldige Musikwissenschaftler notwendig wäre, bleibt das Original immer besser. Einige besondere Stücke der Suiten für Violine, die "vollendete" Suite für Flöte und die Bearbeitungen für Streichtrio (Violine-Viola-Cello) oder für Bläserfanfaren sind ebenfalls mit vollständigen Partituren versehen, um eine leichtere Aufführung zu ermöglichen. Sie alle sind auf den Websites der IMSLP und AIMAmusic zu finden.

4.2   Überraschende versteckte Ragtime Rhythmen

Die rhythmische Komplexität, die in einigen Stücken zu beobachten ist, ist die überraschendste und umstrittenste Seite dieser versteckten dreistimmigen Kanons. Aus der Sicht potenzieller Kritiker könnte man sie als trivialen Trick bezeichnen, um dissonanten Akkorden zu entgehen, weil die

Noten im Takt feiner skaliert sind, und dies mag wie eine Spielerei erscheinen, die der Zeit Bachs nicht angemessen ist. Aber nachdem ich eine ganze Weile nach Lösungen gesucht habe, kann ich Ihnen versichern, dass dieser "Trick" nicht bei allen Stücken funktioniert, und wenn kein anständiger Kanon gefunden werden kann, schafft er nur Verwirrung. Außerdem findet sich die gleiche rhythmische Komplexität der Gegentempi in den von Bach in BWV 1072 vorgeschlagenen pädagogischen Archetypen wieder. Die Konsequenz daraus ist, dass dieser immanente Rhythmus, der für spätere romantische Rhapsodien und Ragtimes des 20. Jahrhunderts typisch ist, von Bach entdeckt und wahrscheinlich nicht gezeigt wurde, weil er für seine Zeit zu modern und sicherlich zu destabilisierend für Hoftänze war, die weit von modernen Tanzsälen entfernt sind.

4.3   *Die Kirchenatmosphäre beim Hören mehrstimmiger Kanons*

Mit Ausnahme der bereits erwähnten Stücke mit amüsanten rhythmischen Effekten schaffen die anderen analysierten Kanonstücke eine Atmosphäre und einen Klang von Kirchenmusik, voller Echos und Resonanzen. Wenn man ihnen zu lange zuhört, ermüden sie aufgrund der Aufmerksamkeit und Konzentration, die ihre Komplexität erfordert. Dies erklärt auch, warum Bach keine expliziten Mehrstimmigerkanonversionen dieser Stücke vorschlug, die mit mehreren Instrumenten gespielt werden sollten, trotz des höheren Gewinns, den er damit erzielt hätte (die Partituren wurden im Verhältnis zu ihrer Länge und der Anzahl der Noten bezahlt!): Sie wären viel weniger geschätzt worden als Versionen für ein einzelnes Instrument. Warum also so viel Mühe aufwenden, um mehrstimmige Kanons zu komponieren und sie gleichzeitig versteckt zu halten? Der zweite Teil des Buches versucht, diese Frage zu beantworten.

TEIL II VERSTEHEN, nicht UNTERSTEHEN

5 Notwendigkeit ist die Mutter der Neuheit

1. Es ist nun an der Zeit zu versuchen zu verstehen, warum J.S. Bach auf diese besondere Weise komponierte und warum er so

Abbild 11 Johann Sebastian Bach (wenn 61) in einem Porträt von Elias Gottlob Haussmann, 1746 auf Leinwand. Bach hält ein Notenblatt des sechsstimmigen Kanons BWV 1076 in der Hand. Public Domain, http://www.jsbach.net/bass/elements/bach-hausmann.jpg , https://commons.wikimedia.org/w/index.php?curid=1270015

stolz darauf war, dass er in seinem Porträt eine Partitur mit mehrstimmigen Kanons in seiner Hand hielt, als Summa seines Lebenswerkes.

Sogar sein Monogramm (Siegel) hat eine Krone in der Mitte: Er war sich bewusst, dass er der König der Kanons war (und für immer sein würde). Bei näherer Betrachtung erkennt man eine Reihe von drei parallelen Linien, die vielleicht an die dreistimmigen, gespiegelten Kanons erinnern, vielleicht auch an die Krebskanons, die noch irgendwo entdeckt werden müssen, …

Fig.12 Bachs bekrontes Siegel, in den Leipzig Jahren angewendet.
Es enthält die Buchstaben J S B in einer gespiegelten und
zusammengepackten Art. Public Domain.
https://commons.wikimedia.org/wiki/File:Bach_Seal.svg#filelinks.

5.1 Das außergewöhnliche Leben von J.S. Bach

Niemand kann auf ein Talent stolz sein, das er von Geburt an hat, aber wenn er es durch hartes Üben und ein hartes Leben entwickelt hat, dann kann er es tatsächlich sein. Johann Sebastian war das jüngste von sieben Kindern und wurde sicherlich von seinen Eltern und Geschwistern verwöhnt und auch von anderen Onkeln, die Musiker waren, erzogen. Er spielte auf verschiedenen Instrumenten, von der Geige bis zum Cembalo, und wuchs unbeschwert in einem kleinen Dorf im Heiligen Römischen Reich des Westens auf. Er war erst neun Jahre alt, als seine Mutter starb und sein Vater starb wenige Monate später auch. Das Paradies der Kindheit war für immer verloren. Sein ältester Bruder hatte glücklicherweise bereits eine

Stelle als Organist an der Michaeliskirche in Ohrdruf und nahm ihn und einen weiteren kleinen Bruder bei sich auf. Die Schule bot sicherlich keinen Schutz (vgl. [13]). Wir können uns nur vorstellen, dass J.S. in diesem neuen Leben in der Kirche Zuflucht fand und von seinem Bruder das Orgelspiel lernte, zum Spaß und um selbst Musiker zu werden. Sicherlich lernte er auswendig, und wenn er konnte, kopierte er alle kostbaren Notenblätter, die im Umlauf waren (auch auf die Gefahr hin, für die Verschwendung von kostbarem Papier bestraft zu werden), um die Musik der mitteldeutschen Komponisten zu entdecken, sie zu spielen und ihre Komponierkunst zu verstehen. Er war intelligent und brillant genug, um für ein Stipendium an der berühmten St. Michaelis Schule in Lüneburg ausgewählt zu werden. Wichtig für uns ist, dass er sicherlich viel Zeit mit dem Spielen der Kirchenorgel verbracht hat und so die autistischen Tendenzen, die durch das Trauma des Waisendaseins verursacht wurden, überwunden hat, denn er wurde ein Meister der Improvisation.

5.2   Raum Akustik als auslösender Kontext

In der Welt J.S. Bachs wurde in lutherischen Tempeln, kahl und streng, oder in den leeren, steingemauerten Sälen von Palästen, die höchstens mit ein paar Wandteppichen geschmückt waren, musiziert. Akustisch zeichneten sich diese beiden Raumtypen durch eine lange Nachhallzeit und wenige dominante Echos aus. In den so genannten Hallenkirchen (mit gleicher Deckenhöhe im Kirchenschiff und in den Seitenschiffen) entsprachen die beiden Hauptechos zum einen der Länge des Kirchenschiffs und zum anderen der konstanten Höhe der Kirche. Das Ergebnis war sicherlich ein gewisses akustisches Chaos und ein sehr schwieriges Hören von Musik und Reden, vor allem bei Entfernungen von mehr als zwei oder drei Metern zu den Musikern oder zu den Kanzeln. Akustisch bessere Räume wären Kreuzgänge, Höfe und öffentliche Plätze gewesen, aber das deutsche Klima beschränkte ihre Nutzung auf die warme

Jahreszeit oder auf Blasinstrumente, die weniger empfindlich auf Temperatur- und Feuchtigkeitsschwankungen reagierten als Instrumente mit Darmsaiten. Die andere akustisch brauchbare Alternative waren die überfüllten Tavernen, aber das waren Orte für Spielleute und Musiker, die kein Komponist in Betracht gezogen hätte (nicht zuletzt, weil er nicht an den Einkünften der Spieler beteiligt gewesen wäre). In den katholischen Kirchen des Barocks wurde dank der Vielfalt an Formen, Kapellen, Nischen, Statuen, Säulen und unzähligen Stuckverzierungen, Holzpaneelen, die als natürliche Diffusoren wirkten, das Auftreten von Echos abgeschwächt, und ein Bachs Genius wäre nie mit diesem Problem in Berührung gekommen. Das Gleiche gilt heute für schallschluckende Platten. Tatsache ist, dass für den jungen Bach, der seine Zeit an der Orgel der Ohrdrufer Kirche (einer Hallenkirche) verbrachte, das größte akustische Problem darin bestand, eine klare, scharfe Musik zu erhalten, indem er gegen die allgegenwärtigen Resonanzen und Rumpelgeräusche, die disharmonischen Überlagerungen, die klangliche Unordnung, diese Verwirrung ankämpfte, die inakzeptabel und unvereinbar mit dem Konzept von Ordnung und Harmonie war, das für seine Religion, für die Leibnizsche Philosophie, die seine Erziehung durchdrang, grundlegend war.

5.3 Die geniale Lösung Bachs

Nachdem ich so viele dreistimmige Kanons entdeckt habe, bin ich zu der **These** gelangt, dass die geniale Lösung, die der junge Bach für das akustische Problem der Echos in den Sälen, in denen er spielte, fand, darin bestand, die Musik so anzupassen, dass eine harmonische Überlagerung mit den Echos erreicht wurde. Eine Art Synergie enstand zwischen den Echos und dem Klang der Instrumente. Diese Synergie führte zur Bekämpfung vom Wirrwarr des diffusen und halligen Feldes, das ein unzusammenhängendes Hintergrundgeräusch darstellte.
Um zu dieser Entdeckung zu gelangen, waren **zwei außergewöhnliche Gaben** erforderlich. Die erste ist eine große

Begabung für die Anpassung der eigenen Musikdarbietung an äußere Klangereignisse, auch bekannt als geschulte Improvisation. Dieser intensive Wunsch nach Neuem und die Fähigkeit, frei zu improvisieren, wurde ihm durch die *Langeweile* geweckt, nachdem er die Noten seines Bruders erkundet, ausgebeutet und ausgeschöpft hatte.

Die zweite ist die Entwicklung eines ungewöhnlichen Gehörs, mit einer manisch-autistischen Aufmerksamkeit für Echos und für die Gesamtwirkung der Musik in einem bestimmten Raum. Diese Aufmerksamkeit nicht nur für die Töne, die das Instrument von sich gibt, dieses allwissende Hören, das in der Kirche von Ohrdruf ausgebrütet wurde, war ein Geschenk der *Einsamkeit* und der Stille.

J.S. Bachs berühmte Improvisation fasst die reiche melodische Vorstellungskraft zu seiner extremen auditiven Kontrolle: Er hatte die Begabung zu hören, wie die drei Musikelemente zusammen klingen/wirken, das gespielte Element, das Echo von dem vorhergespielten, und das noch zu spielende Element. Diese Aufführungsart entspricht dem Wesen des Kanons und der beiden Anklänge an die dreistimmigen Kanons von Hallenkirchen.

Zeit und Raum. Analysiert man die verborgenen Kanons in den verschiedenen Suiten Bachs (den französischen und englischen Suiten oder den Suiten für Cello, Violine oder Flöte), so stellt man fest, dass die Verzögerung zwischen den Stimmen im Allgemeinen zwischen einer Viertel- und einer halben Sekunde variiert, was einer Kirchenschiffslänge von vierzig bis achtzig Metern entspricht, was sehr plausibel ist. In den ersten Orgelstücken, die Bach geschrieben hat, z.B. der Fuge in C BWV Anh.107 oder der Fantasia in C-Dur BWV 570, sind ebenfalls Kanons versteckt. Das stützt meine folgende Theorie ganz gut: Ich gehe davon aus, dass Bachs Gehörbildung und erste Improvisationserfahrungen in Ohrdruf stattgefunden haben, während die bewusste Ausarbeitung und technische Verfeinerung, in den folgenden Studienjahren, in Lüneburg, und in den frühen Jahren seines Wirkens erfolgten. Ich hatte noch nicht das Vergnügen, die Kompositionen von Dieterich Buxtehude zu analysieren, den Bach in Lüneburg ausspioniert hatte und der die Struktur der Fuge intensiv nutzte, aber ich glaube nicht, dass ich darin einen versteckten mehrstimmigen Kanon finden kann: Er ist sicherlich eine Erfindung Bachs, die auf seiner Lebenserfahrung beruht. Die auf immanenten (verborgenen) Kanons basierende Aufführungstechnik erklärt auch J.S. Bachs Erfolg bei Improvisationswettbewerben: Er passte den von ihm ausgestrahlten Klang an den Klang an, der in den Raum zurückkehrte, was zu reichhaltigen Harmonien, klaren und scharfen Klängen führte. Dies wurde zur geheimen Zutat von J.S. Bachs Kompositionen, und vielleicht versuchte er, es zu lehren und an seine Frau und Kinder weiterzugeben, wie man in BWV 1072-86 und 1087 sehen kann, die das Geheimnis bis ins Grab trugen.

Diese Hypothese des akustischen Ziels des klaren und scharfen Hörens in diffusen Feldern mit Echos, das Bach mit den Kanons erreicht hat, wurde zufällig bestätigt, als ich ein Orgelkonzert in einer großen Kirche mit sehr schlechter Akustik hörte: Nur Bachs Stücke hoben sich scharf von dem verworrenen Hintergrundgeräusch ab, die Stücke anderer Komponisten gingen in den Echos unter.

Zur weiteren Untermauerung muss ich erwähnen, dass Bach großes **Interesse am Phänomen des Echos** zeigte: viele seiner Kompositionen sind mit Echos überschrieben (in BVW 821, 831, 1002). Es sei darauf hingewiesen, dass das Interesse an Echos und deren Verwendung in Musikstücken bereits in der Renaissance bei H. Vecchi, A. Banchieri, G. Gabrieli... zu finden ist, oder in der Zeit, die näher an Bach liegt, bei I. Posch, G. Scronx (*Echo in F-Dur* 1617), S. Scheidt (*Echo ad manuale duplex* 1624), C. de Tallard (*Air in Echo*, Suite pour Lute) und später bei A. Lotti (Sonata a 4: *Echo-Adagio-Presto* 1717), A.

Vivaldi (RV552, *Concerto con violino principale con altro per eco* 1740) und bei Dutzenden jüngerer Komponisten der Musikgeschichte, aber man kann sehen, dass Bach der unbestrittene König über sie alle ist.

Als J.S. Bach für den Bau und die Stimmung der Mühlhausener **Orgel** verantwortlich war, versuchte er mehrmals, einige **Glocken hinzuzufügen**. Diese Idee mag überraschend erscheinen: Die Orgel verfügt bereits über mehrere Klaviaturen und Register und ist reich an verschiedenen Klangfarben und Klängen. Diese Idee stammte von der Arnstädter Orgel mit dem Cymbelstern, aber im Gegensatz zum Cymbelstern, der sich automatisch drehte und die Glocken mit der aus den Pfeifen strömenden Luft auf zufällige und chaotische Weise bewegte, wollte Bach, dass die Glocken von einer Klaviatur gesteuert werden, die von Hämmern wie die Saiten eines Cembalos gespielt wird. Abgesehen von seiner Vorliebe für Ordnung und Präzision ist meine Interpretation als Akustiker, dass er einen ganz anderen Klang als die Orgel brauchte, mit einem sehr präzisen Anschlag im Takt, um sich an die Echos in der Kirche anzupassen und seine Improvisationen mit versteckten Kanons zu bewältigen.

Nun ein **Vorgeschmack von Umständlichkeit**: der wissenschaftliche Einwand gegen diese These könnte lauten, dass die verschiedenen Echos im Allgemeinen nicht in regelmäßigen Zeitabständen zurückkommen, insbesondere wenn die Größe des Raums oder der Abstand zwischen Schallquelle und Wänden nicht gleich sind. Ich kann nur vermuten, dass in der Kirche von Ohrdruf die Position der Orgel und die Abmessungen die richtige waren: wenn sich die Orgel zum Beispiel am Ende des Kirchenschiffs befand und das Kirchenschiff doppelt so lang war wie die Kirchenhöhe, dann waren die Echos auf die gleiche Raumgröße zurückzuführen und kamen mit einer konstanten Zeitverzögerung zu seinen Ohren zurück.

Lassen Sie mich noch eine letzte pingelige Bemerkung machen: Das serielle Komponieren von Meisterwerken mit versteckten Kanons gehört eindeutig zur **Zeit in Weimar** (1708-1717), daher vermute ich, dass Bach dort auch in der Musik mit Echoproblemen konfrontiert war, die denen der Ohrdrufer Kirche ähneln; z.B. in den Räumen des Herzogspalastes, da die meisten Stücke, die ich analysiert habe, eher für „Kammermusik" als für Kirchenmusik komponiert sind. Bachs Orgelwerk sollte deshalb besser analysiert werden, um versteckte Kanons zu finden und meine These zu bestätigen. Wenn jedoch nichts gefunden wird, würde das bedeuten, dass die Intuition darüber, wie versteckte Kanons verwendet wurden, nicht mit der Kirchenzeit von Ohrdruf, sondern mit der von Weimar zusammenhängt. Was aus akustischer Sicht effektiver wäre, da man in einem Palastkonzertsaal den richtigen Ort zum Spielen wählen kann, was mit einer Kirchenorgel nicht möglich ist.

6 Akustisches Gedächtnis und psychoakustische Wirkung

6.1 *Das akustische Gedächtnis*

Nach grundlegenden Konzepten der Psychoakustik ist das akustische Gedächtnis normaler Menschen sehr kurz, vor allem in Bezug auf unsinnige Geräusche: Wenn man beispielsweise die Geräusche von zwei Fahrzeugkonfigurationen vergleichen will, muss man sie in dichter Folge proben oder über Kopfhörer aufnehmen und vergleichen. Für andere Geräusche, die mit dem menschlichen Überleben zu tun haben, ist das Gehör dank der physiologischen Evolution viel empfindlicher und kann kleine Abweichungen von den gewohnten Umgebungsgeräuschen wahrnehmen, vom Geräusch einer Mücke über das Knirschen eines trockenen Blattes bis hin zur Fehlfunktion einer Maschine.

Im Allgemeinen ist das Gehirn präziser und aufmerksamer, wenn eine Information oder ein Gefühl mit dem Hören verbunden ist. Apropos geschulte Ohren: Manche Musiker haben kein Problem damit, 24-Oktaven-Intervalle (Vierteltöne) zu unterscheiden oder sich eine Melodie oder ein komplexes Musikstück in Bezug auf Frequenzen (Harmonien) und zeitliche Abläufe (Rhythmen) zu merken, und manche können sich Frequenzen absolut merken oder beurteilen, ob die Tonamplitude im Laufe der Zeit zu- oder abgenommen hat.

Dadurch sind sie in der Lage, ihre Vortragsdynamik in Bezug auf Amplitude und Geschwindigkeit anzupassen. Sie können sich auch ganze Stunden von Musik merken. Das Gleiche gilt für Schauspieler mit Gedichten oder Theatertexten und für viele religiöse Menschen mit auswendig gelernten Büchern mit heiligen Texten.

Andererseits ist zu beobachten, dass auch ungeübte Menschen sich Melodien oder kurze Gedichte oder Sätze merken können, die sie gerade gehört haben, und dass die Interpretation des Gehörten Zeit braucht, zum Beispiel bei Reden, wenn mehrere Personen gleichzeitig sprechen und man allen Reden folgen muss. Mit anderen Worten kann man sagen, dass der nützliche Klang für eine gewisse Zeit im Gehirn "lebendig" gehalten wird, als ob er in einem Hallraum, in einer Art interpretativem Gedächtnisraum, nachhallen würde. Um auf Bachs Welt zurückzukommen, kann man beobachten (und Charlie Chaplin hat das im „Großen Diktator" großartig gemacht!), dass die grammatikalische Struktur deutscher Sätze, die die Sinnbestimmung bis zum letzten Verb aufschiebt, ein längeres interpretatives Gedächtnis erfordert. Diese systematische und unbewusste Verarbeitungszeit in unserem Gehirn gibt es sowohl für Sprache als auch für Musik: Das bedeutet, dass, *während wir einen Klang hören, der vorherige Klang in unserem Gedächtnis präsent ist* und mitschwingt.

6.2   Bachs zweite Intuition

Ich denke, dass Bach diese geistige Dynamik zur Zeit von Ohrdruf (der ideale Ortsname für seine Gehörberufung!) beobachtet und verstanden hat. Ich stelle die Hypothese auf, dass er ein Phänomen, das für andere unbewusst ist, in einen bewussten und kontrollierten Zustand brachte und es nutzte, um seine Improvisationswettbewerbe zu gewinnen und harmonische Effekte und außergewöhnliche Empfindungen in den Gehirnen der Zuhörer zu erzielen, wo die Musik sich dank des interpretativen Gedächtnisses selbst begleitet und bereichert. Da das akustische Interpretationsgedächtnis nicht von der physischen Anwesenheit von Echos am Hörplatz abhängt, betrifft die Wirksamkeit von Bachs Ansatz die allgemeine Hörerfahrung. Dieser zweite Teil meiner These könnte daher als Negation des ersten Teils gesehen werden: kein Echoproblem, das es zu lösen gilt, keine Raumakustik, nur psychoakustische Gehirnfunktionen und Bachs geniale Intuition.

Ich ziehe es vor zu glauben, dass beide Erklärungen nebeneinander bestehen, denn ich mag beide und bin nicht monogam mit Ideen. Ich habe die physikalische Erklärung (Raumakustik) persönlich erlebt, und die zweite (die psychoakustische) ist theoretisch schwieriger zu beweisen (ich habe noch keine Musikwissenschaftler viviseziert!), aber Sie können sie selbst erleben, indem Sie sich auf das konzentrieren, was Sie hören und was in Ihrem Gedächtnis nachklingt, während Sie Bachs Stücke hören.

Selbst wenn man nur die psychische Erklärung berücksichtigt, bleibt die Empfehlung, beim Spielen dieser Bach-Stücke ein gleichmäßiges Tempo beizubehalten, in jedem Fall gültig.

6.3   Die Strategie hinter den verborgenen Kanons

Als ich zum ersten Mal die drei- oder siebenstimmigen Kanons in den Suiten (für Cello, Violine oder Flöte) entdeckte, dachte ich, es handele sich um eine geniale Strategie Bachs, um die Wirkung eines polyphonen Konzerts mit nur einem Melodieinstrument zu erzielen, was für die Hofreisen des Fürsten Leopold von Köthen sehr nützlich und wirtschaftlich war. Dies war wahrscheinlich ein "Nebeneffekt", denn ich wusste noch nicht, dass Bach in seinen früheren Weimarer Werken, den Englischen und Französischen Suiten für Cembalo, mehrstimmige Kanons versteckt hatte! Hinzu kommt, dass er auch später noch für größere Besetzungen komponieren sollte: Mehrere Konzerte für Orchester und Solisten enthalten versteckte mehrstimmige Kanons. Die "Reisekoffer"-Hypothese fiel also völlig in sich zusammen, und es musste eine Erklärung gefunden werden: Die bereits früher aufgestellte These über die Wirkung von Klarheit und Schärfe des Klangs in feindlicher Umgebung (Raumakustik) und die Bereicherung der Hörempfindungen (Psychoakustik).

6.4   Warum so lange versteckt?

Die Suiten für Soloinstrumente sind die Stücke von Bach, in denen man die verborgenen Kanons am leichtesten entdecken kann; das ist mir als Cellist passiert, aber auch dank der Leidenschaft für die Analyse von Texten und historisch-philosophischen Zusammenhängen, die mir mein Onkel vererbt hat, dem Interesse an Religion und Psychologie, das mir mein Vater vererbt hat, dem wissenschaftlichen Verständnis für akustische Phänomene, das mir ein Doktortitel vermittelte, der technischen Vertrautheit mit Computern, einer metamusikalischen kontrapunktischen Kompositionsmethode [11] und einer gewissen autistischen Beharrlichkeit. Es ist immer das Ergebnis, das Resultat, das alle notwendigen Elemente auf unvorhersehbare, widersprüchliche und unwahrscheinliche Weise auf sich zieht. Fürst Leopold hätte als guter Calvinist von Prädestination gesprochen, von einem notwendigen Universum.

Warum ist niemandem dieser mehrstimmige Kanon aufgefallen, der drei Jahrhunderte lang in Bachs Melodien versteckt war? Ich werde versuchen, einige mögliche Erklärungen zu geben: Die Tanzsuiten waren eine Form, die nicht mehr gebraucht wurde, die Hoftänze, flüchtig und alltäglich, veränderten sich, die von Bach vorgeschlagenen waren unbrauchbar, dann verlagerte sich die Musik für Soloinstrumente von den Höfen in die bürgerlichen Salons, gepolstert und ohne Echo, Bachs Stücke, Symbole des Gleichgewichts und der Harmonie, waren zwar virtuos, aber nicht romantisch genug und für Straßenmusiker waren die Partituren zu teuer.

Die Bachs Suiten wurden von großen Komponisten wie Mendelssohn studiert, und Bachs Musik beeinflusste Haydn, Mozart, Beethoven und viele spätere Komponisten, aber niemand bemerkte die auf dem Porträt gezeigten raffinierten Kanons. Die Fuge schien für einen Komponisten und Musikwissenschaftler komplexer und anspruchsvoller zu sein. Dieses Vergessen offenbart auch, dass keiner von Bachs Verwandten jemals die geheime Zutat des "Familienbetriebes“ preisgegeben hat, trotz Anna Magdalenas Armut: Sie haben es wahrscheinlich geschworen oder wussten es nicht. Man müsste ihre Stücke studieren ...

Selbst in unserer spätromantischen Epoche haben Solisten wie Casals oder Glenn Gould, die ihr Leben mit den Suiten verbrachten, deren Schönheit ausgenutzt, um ihr Talent zum Ausdruck zu bringen, ohne zu bemerken, welche Schätze sie verbargen. Andererseits ist es schwierig, sich von der Anziehungskraft und dem Vergnügen, das sie beim Spielen hervorrufen, zu lösen, denn die Melodien ändern sich ständig in Stil und Atmosphäre und können nicht als kanonisch angesehen werden.

6.5 Letzte Über-arbeitung/raschung der Suiten

Nachdem ich die physikalische Erklärung für das Spiel mit den Echos formuliert hatte, stellte ich meine frühere Analyse der Cellosuiten in Frage: Die zeitlichen Verzögerungen der Stimmen waren, im Vergleich zu den Suiten, die ich später analysierte, und im Vergleich zur Größe der Räume zu lang. So fand ich Lösungen mit kürzeren Verzögerungen, die **keine Veränderungen in den Präludien der zweiten und der ersten Suite** zur Folge hatten. Alle Vermutungen über die "Löcher" in den Abschnitten 2.5 und 2.6, die Bach in den Partituren hinterlassen und Anna Magdalena vervollständigt hat, sind mit diesen neuen Lösungen nicht mehr notwendig, obwohl sie verführerisch und amüsant sind. Der Anfang der zweiten Suite wird somit:

Das ganze Werk wäre also aus einem *Hörfehler* beim Präludium der zweiten Suite entstanden, und zwar nach dem Brauch, Kanons mit einer Verzögerung von etwa einem Takt zu singen: ein *fruchtbarer Fehler*, ohne den die echten Kanons nicht zum Vorschein gekommen wären. Ich habe verschiedene Stücke neu analysiert und die neuen Versionen der Partituren auf die Websites von IMSLP und AIMAmusic gestellt.

Es ist auch anzumerken, dass die kurzen Verzögerungen zwischen den Stimmen die Überschneidungen zwischen den verschiedenen Tonalitäten auf kürzere Musikabschnitte beschränken und die Komposition von mehrstimmigen evolutionären und modulierenden Kanons erleichtern. Das Hören der kurzen Verzögerungen ist nicht intuitiv, es ist schwierig und bringt das außergewöhnliche Gehör von J.S. Bach zum Vorschein.

7 Schlussfolgerungen

1.   Ich habe einen verborgenen Schatz gefunden, indem ich der lebendigen Schatzkarte einer Partitur gefolgt bin, nach Jahrhunderten geduldigen Wartens des Komponisten: Kostbare mehrstimmige evolutionäre und modulierende Kanons sind wie Diamanten und Smaragde eingebettet, immanent, unsichtbar, in vielen von J.S. Bachs Meisterwerken.

2.   Indem ich dies "en passant" tat, verstand ich den Sinn der seltsamen Reise meines Lebens besser.

3.   Jetzt kann jeder die Komplexität von Bachs Werk hören, seine verfremdenden Meisterwerke wiederentdecken und neue Fähigkeiten des eigenen Geistes erkunden.

4.   Musiker können zusammen oder allein mit Audiounterstützung spielen und neue Wege der Interpretation von Klassikern finden. Sogar das Klonen von Musikern kann jetzt Sinn machen!

5.   Musiker können vorsichtiger wählen, wo sie spielen oder Bachs Musik in einem akustisch ungünstigen Raum hören.

6.   Musikwissenschaftler können Bachs Werke weiter erforschen und andere unerwartete Welten entdecken oder Zeit damit verschwenden, dieses Werk für ungültig zu erklären, wenn es ihnen gefällt.

7.   Und wenn es nur ein Traum war, so war es doch ein wunderbarer Traum, der es wert war, geträumt zu werden!

Verborgene Kanons Noten

[A] Cello Suites https://imslp.org/wiki/File:PMLP4291-6CelloSuitesHiddenCanonsGuide.pdf

[B] Violin Suites best of
https://imslp.org/wiki/Special:ImagefromIndex/790271/vg25

[C] "completed" Flute Suite
https://imslp.org/wiki/Special:ImagefromIndex/788474/vg25

[D] "completed" French Suites
https://imslp.org/wiki/Special:ImagefromIndex/809911/vg25

[E] English Suites
https://imslp.org/wiki/Special:ImagefromIndex/809741/vg25

[F] Goldberg Variations Aria
https://imslp.org/wiki/Special:ImagefromIndex/809278/vg25

[G] Violin Concerto BWV 1041
https://imslp.org/wiki/Special:ImagefromIndex/821336/vg25

[H] 2 Violins Concerto BWV 1043
https://imslp.org/wiki/Special:ImagefromIndex/821337/vg25

[I] Oboe and Violin Concerto BWV 1060R
https://imslp.org/wiki/Special:ImagefromIndex/821335/vg25

[J] 5th Brandenburger BWV 1050 Allegro
https://imslp.org/wiki/Special:ImagefromIndex/822690/vg25

HoerBeispiele auf YouTube (und anderes)

https://www.youtube.com/channel/UCG4BI8Q1vR7SbMxCxDJ_yIA

https://metamusica.altervista.org/

Kleinste Bibliographie

[1.a] Denis Collins, *From Bull to Bach: In Search of Precedents for the "Complete" Version of the Canon by Augmentation and Contrary Motion in J. S. Bach's "Musical Offering"* Source: Bach, Vol. 38, No. 2 (2007), pp. 39-63 Published by: Riemenschneider Bach Institute.

[1.b] Dennis Collins and W. Andrew Schloss, *An Unusual Effect in the Canon Per Tonos from J. S. Bach's Musical Offering* Source: Music Perception: An Interdisciplinary Journal, Vol. 19, No. 2 (Winter 2001), pp. 141-153 Published by: University of California Press

[1.c] Denis Collins, *Bach and Approaches to Canonic Composition in Early Eighteenth-Century Theoretical and Chamber Music Sources*. Source: Bach, Vol. 30, No. 2 (1999), pp. 27-48 Published by: Riemenschneider Bach Institute

[2] Marcel Bitsch , *J.S. Bach, canons BWV 1087: analyse et commentaires* 1977, Durand, T. Presse

[3] Christoph Wolff, "Bach's Handexemplar of the Goldberg Variations: A New Source", Journal of the American Musicological Society XXIV/2 (Summer 1976), pp. 224-241.

[4] Denis Collins *Historical precedents for Bach's "evolutio" canon BWV1087/10* Source: Bach, vol. 24, No. 1 (Spring-Summer, 1993), pp. 5-14 Published by: Riemenschneider Bach Institute

[5] Alexander Maykapar, September 2, 2015 THE 13th CANON: Portrait of J.S. Bach In https://www.projectawe.org/blog?category=AWE https://www.projectawe.org/blog?category=maria+danova

[6a] Athanase Papadopoulos, Mathématiques *et musique chez J.S. Bach*, 2000, L'ouvert 100, papadopoulos@math.u-strasbg.fr

[6b] Martin Jarvis, *Written by Mrs Bach*, 2011, HarperCollins Publishers Australia. http://www.harpercollins.com.au/9780733328725/

[7] Tony Phillips, *Math and the Musical Offering*, https://www.ams.org/publicoutreach/feature-column/fcarc-canons

[8] J.S. Bach Crab Canon on a Moebius band https://www.openculture.com/2009/09/how_a_bach_canon_works.html

[9a] Denis Collins, *Bach's Occasional Canon BWV 1073 and "Stacked" Canonic Procedure in the Eighteenth Century* Source: Bach, Vol. 33, No. 2 (2002), pp. 15-34 Published by: Riemenschneider Bach Institute

[9b] Albert Clement, *Johann Sebastian Bach and the praise of God, some thoughts on the canon triplex (BWV 1076),* In: Music and theology: essays in honor of Robin A. Leaver/ed. by Daniel Zager-Lanham, Md.[u.a.], 2007.- S. 147-168

[10] Dr. Timothy A. Smith, Northern Arizona University *Canons and Fugues of J.S. Bach*, Tutorial 2020-2021

[11] https://metamusica.altervista.org/spiegazioni/generalinfo.html

[12] Bob van Asperen, contrib. F. Huneau, M. Quagliozzi, *François Dieupart's Biography Revised and the Genesis and Dating of his Six Suittes de Clavessin, with Remarks on their Influence on J.S. Bach.* Amsterdam, 2021

[13] John Eliot Gardiner, *Bach: Music in the Castle of Heaven,* 2013

Über den Autor

Giovanni Pietro Orefice (Milano 1967-Gap-Grenoble-Lyon-Berlin-Paris-Torino-Milano/Desenzano/Modena), PhD in Akustik, Cellist, Komponist von Metamusik (s. [11]).

I segreti dei canoni nascosti nei capolavori di J.S. Bach

Büchlein für Johann Sebastian

Introduzione

Ascoltando la musica del sommo compositore J.S. Bach chiunque può sentire una profonda risonanza delle sue melodie nella propria anima. Inoltre, se in una chiesa riverberante si confrontano i suoi capolavori per organo a quelli di altri compositori risaltano per chiarezza in modo impressionante. In questo piccolo libro proverò ad approfondire e spiegare entrambe queste esperienze, basandomi sul recente lavoro che ho svolto per svelare i canoni nascosti in molti pezzi famosi di J.S. Bach e che presenterò in dettaglio.

Ho cercato di scrivere questo testo in un modo comprensibile e semplice, evitando il più possibile i tecnicismi degli articoli specialistici di musicologia. Lo scopo è di ispirare musicisti e musicologi, fornendo loro molti spunti per ricerche più ortodosse e di essere una guida per tutti gli appassionati della musica di Bach, che scopriranno nei pezzi indicati nei links la bellezza dei canoni multipli e troveranno una spiegazione delle sensazioni indescrivibili che provano quando ascoltano le sue opere.

In barba a qualunque aspettativa, dopo tre secoli dalla sua composizione l'opera di J.S. Bach serba ancora molte sorprese e tesori nascosti. La prima parte di questo libricino presenta il lavoro esteso di ricerca musicologica che ho svolto su un mostro sacro della storia della musica come J.S. Bach, per svelare la struttura immanente di canone multiplo nascosta nella sua opera, finora sconosciuta. Come violoncellista ho cominciato questa scoperta dalle Suite a Violoncello solo, proseguendo sulle Sonate e Partite per violino solo, sulla Suite incompleta per

Flauto, sulle Suite Francesi e Inglesi per clavicembalo, aggiungendo qualche Preludio a completamento e ho terminato esplorando qualche concerto per orchestra e strumenti solistici. Nell'esporre questo lavoro evidenzierò degli effetti ritmici inattesi e delle parti incompiute/mancanti in alcuni pezzi, proponendo qualche pista per completarli e qualche soluzione a vecchie dispute e a problemi di attribuzione. Cercherò di spiegare la complessità/difficoltà del comporre canoni multipli e fornirò qualche paragone con pezzi di altri autori famosi dell'epoca per fare nuova luce sul talento e le capacità fuori dal comune di J.S. Bach, ancora sottostimate.

Nella seconda parte del libro presenterò una tesi innovativa, che combina le conoscenze di fisica acustica e psicoacustica dei miei studi e della mia professione, con la mia esperienza e riflessione di musicista esecutore. Questo approccio peculiare fornisce una spiegazione dei motivi pratici e tattici di J.S. Bach per nascondere in modo pervasivo nelle sue linee melodiche i canoni multipli presentati nella prima parte. Questa teoria permette di chiarire come Bach abbia risolto, come improvvisatore e compositore alcuni problemi tipici degli esecutori traendone un vantaggio competitivo nei suoi famosi e gloriosi tornei di improvvisazione. La tesi sostiene inoltre che Bach capì istintivamente alcuni effetti psicoacustici e decise di adottare questo ingrediente segreto per comporre capolavori e ottenere un successo mondiale imperituro.

Se non siete interessati ai dettagli tecnici delle strutture dei canoni e alle tappe del processo di scoperta dei canoni nascosti, ma volete capire perché J.S. Bach li nascondeva, saltate direttamente alla seconda parte, al capitolo 5, ma leggere qualche pagina in più non vi ucciderà!

PARTE I   CANONI, non CANNONI
1   Canoni espliciti e casi nascosti, immanenti

Per i dettagli della scoperta dei canoni nascosti saltate al capitolo 2. Lo scopo di questo capitolo è di fare la distinzione tra i canoni espliciti e visibili nelle composizioni di Bach e quelli nascosti che saranno trattati nel secondo capitolo.

Visione abituale dei canoni di J.S. Bach

I canoni più famosi e sviluppati di Bach sono i dieci scritti esplicitamente nell'Offerta Musicale BWV 1079 per il re di Prussia, cf [1], dei quali Anton von Webern orchestrò il Ricercare a 6 voci nel 1935. Bach scrisse anche la variazione a canone su "Von Himmel hoch" (per organo) BWV 769 come lettera di presentazione per la Mizler Society di Lipsia, della quale divenne membro nel 1747. Queste due opere mostrano quanto importante fosse la forma del canone per lui e quanto stimasse la sua abilità nel destreggiarsi con essa, tanto da considerarla il suo biglietto da visita e addirittura un presente degno di un monarca. D'altro canto troviamo un canone perfino nel libricino (Büchlein) per Anna Magdalena (Canon, BWV Anh.120), eletto in questo modo a sommo pegno d'amore.

Accanto ai pezzi musicali precedenti, i suoi canoni brevi BWV 1072-86 sono considerati e classificati generalmente come materiale pedagogico per i suoi figli e allievi, o come esercizi / pezzi di circostanza (BWV 1073), o, al contrario, santificati (canon triplex BWV 1076) [9]. Vediamo per esempio il primo canone nella Fig.1.

Figura 1: BWV 1072 Kanon zu acht Stimmen. Si può osservare qui che la linea melodica oscilla, come un'onda sinusoidale e che quattro voci stanno all'interno delle battute mentre altre quattro voci (intermedie) hanno note a cavallo e creano una certa complessità ritmica in controtempo. Gli stessi elementi si possono ripetere all'infinito (canone circolare).Una nona voce sarebbe identica alla prima.

Anche nell'Arte della Fuga WV 1080 Bach mostrava chiaramente canoni a 4 voci e strutture complesse ("canon alla duodecima in contrappunto alla quinta; due canoni per augmentationem in contrario motu") e non sono considerati meri esercizi, ma pezzi di musica a tutti gli effetti.

La scoperta dei 14 Canoni BWV 1087, una sola pagina (c.f. Fig.2), trovati solo nel 1974 alla fine della copia personale di Bach delle Variazioni Goldberg BWV988, svelò al mondo quanto la struttura di canone potesse essere raffinata e complessa nella sua mente, con varianti a simmetria orizzontale e verticale (sullo spartito) e l'esplorazione di dilatazioni e dimezzamenti del tempo, in aggiunta allo slittamento nel tempo tipico dei canoni.

Questo foglio è una vera Guida ai canoni, largamente spiegata, discussa e illustrata, c.f. [2], [3], [4], [5]. Inoltre il 13° canone corrisponde a quello rappresentato nel ritratto di J.S. Bach fatto da Elias Gottlob Haussmann (1746), quindi questa preziosa pagina conteneva quello che lui considerava il più importante lascito della sua vita: un testamento musicale!

Figura 2: BWV 1087 Holograph manuscript, n.d.(ca.1741-46)
https://imslp.org/wiki/File:PMLP326356-N55005962_(BWV_1087).pdf

Come "conseguenza", o effetto secondario di questa scoperta, alcuni "studi" (come [6a], [7], [8]) apparvero sulle trasformate matematiche che descrivono i processi di scrittura dei canoni: ma questi lavori possono al più essere usati per sviluppare nuovi strumenti nei software di ausilio alla composizione e non apportano nessuna conoscenza musicale/musicologica interessante.

Nel 1867 Helfer, Friedrich August col suo *Canon für 2 Clav. u. Pedal BACH über Bach,* In: Album für die Orgel zu J. G.Töpfer's goldner Amts-Jubelfeier am 4. Juni 1867. - Weimar: T. F. A. Kühn, 1867, pag. 54-55, ha esplorato un canone nascosto in un pezzo d'organo.

Nonostante tutte queste pubblicazioni la capacità di J.S. Bach di comporre canoni multipli nei suoi capolavori è stata solo assaggiata nel 10° pezzo dell'Offerta Musicale BWV 1079 (*Canon a 4 quaerendo invenietis*) e non è stata mai scoperta ed apprezzata durante la sua vita: il bellicoso re di Prussia non fu molto impressionato durante la sua visita, forse gli era stato promesso un esperto di canoni e aveva frainteso con i suoi beneamati cannoni da guerra!

Più seriamente gli insegnamenti teorici di J.S. Bach lasciati nelle sopracitate lezioni, guide e libretti per i suoi diletti figli e moglie non sembravano avere avuto piena applicazione nei suoi pezzi principali e la sua stima dei canoni come somma forma di creazione non fu mai capita pienamente...

Finora ho solo parlato dei canoni espliciti, visibili nelle diverse opere, più o meno facili da sentire e riconoscere (certamente adesso, grazie ai video pedagogici [10]) e molto conosciuti dai musicologi e da molti musicisti. Il tema di questo libro sono al contrario i canoni immanenti, insospettabili, sconosciuti e nascosti in molte opere, rimasti segreti e che riporto alla luce del nostro intelletto dopo tre secoli di inattenzioni difficilmente spiegabili e abbastanza imperdonabili.

2 Il disvelamento dei canoni nascosti di Bach: un viaggio appassionato

2.1 *Qualche parola sulle Suites di J.S. Bach*

La Suite di danze è una forma musicale che riflette una doppia influenza francese su J.S. Bach. Quella più evidente è il fascino che provava (lui e più generalmente l'insieme delle piccole corti germanofone) per la grande corte del Re Sole Luigi XIV, con le sue danze che davano una rappresentazione fisica della dominazione assoluta del Re sui nobili e sulle dame di corte. Un'altra influenza più sottile è quella filosofica, che partendo da Descartes (e passando da un più complesso Spinoza) arrivò a Leibniz, che sicuramente dominava il pensiero e le credenze in area tedesca al tempo di Bach: la necessità di un'armonia universale, il senso di un universo strutturato, pieno di ordine e bellezza, che riflette la perfezione del suo divino creatore. Nei territori di Bach l'ordine era apprezzato e guidato dall'austera Chiesa di Lutero e Calvino (specialmente austera dopo il terribile periodo dello sterminio degli Anabattisti), opposta al ben diverso, incoerente, lasco mondo della Chiesa cattolica italica, che però aveva qualche lato pieno di fantasia ed improvvisazione, di ornamenti virtuosi ed effetti speciali, di concerti grossi e barocchi che sicuramente affascinavano e ispiravano Bach nelle sue composizioni ed improvvisazioni.

La Suite di danze barocca comincia con una Ouverture, seguita da una alternanza di danze di diversa intensità e velocità, per dosare lo sforzo fisico ed evitare il sudore plebeo. Tipicamente troviamo l'Allemanda, la Corrente, la Sarabande e la Giga. Dopo il 17° secolo altre danze furono integrate ed inserite, come I Minuetti, le Bourrées, le Gavotte, le Passepieds, I Rigaudons ... Per quanto riguarda le Suites per violoncello un famoso precursore e riferimento fu Marin Marais (1656-1728) con le sue *Pièces de viole*, che influenzarono sicuramente il lavoro Bach: il primo libro di queste Pièces (1686) era infatti una Suite completissima (Prelude – Fantaisie – Allemande – Double – Courante – Double – Sarabande – Gigue – Double) e spiega l'uso di Bach dei nomi "Double" e "Phantasie" nelle sue composizioni. La *Suitte d'un Goût Étranger* diMarin Marais concatenava addirittura 33 danze!

Bach aggiunse sempre un paio di "danze galanti" nelle Suites per violoncello, o raddoppiò un altro pezzo come la Courante, o inserì una coppia di pezzi gemelli chiamati "Doubles", o una danza esotica come la Siciliana, o ancora omettendo il nome (lui, o sua moglie, o un copista) di alcuni pezzi delle Partite e Sonate per Violino lasciando solo l'indicazione di velocità/carattere (Presto, Adagio, Largo, Allegro etc.…).

J.S. Bach, come Marin Marais, propose le sue Suites per strumento solo come geniale forma di intrattenimento di una piccola corte, nello stile ideale della sfarzosa Versailles, ma con la modesta spesa di un solo musicista per una intera sessione di danze, come nelle corti rinascimentali, con i loro menestrelli girovaghi. Imperdibili in Bach sono i Preludi, spesso arricchiti dalla complessità di una Fuga, per il loro interesse musicale col loro duplice ruolo di preparazione ai balli e di intrattenimento per un convivio di persone che discutono, come il moderno "piano bar". Accanto all'aspetto formale di queste danze, il lavoro prezioso di Bach trasmette in modo chiaro la sua struttura robusta e presenta delle melodie che penetrano nell'anima di chi le ascolta e traducono in suono la bellezza dell'universo. Ci sono svariate discussioni tra musicologi sullo stile delle danze, se più italiano o francese, ma la cosa importante è l'intento globale e ideale delle Suites: anche le "Suites Inglesi" furono composte e offerte con l'intenzione e la speranza di essere apprezzate nella Corte Inglese, ma sempre per ricreare l'atmosfera e lo splendore della Corte Francese.

Possiamo anche distinguere tra le Suites per clavicembalo, strumento polifonico, autosufficiente e a se stante, composte prima del periodo di Köthen, e quelle per

Violoncello/Violino/Flauto solo, che rappresentavano una sfida compositiva (lanciata da Marin Marais), perché dovevano animare una sessione di danze usando un solo strumento melodico, col problema di trasmettere il ritmo, cosa che era più in uso nella musica di strada, nelle taverne o sulle navi, che nelle Corti principesche dove ma rischiavano di essere inadeguate. Si può ipotizzare che queste Suites possano essere nate come "set da viaggio" per il girovago Prince Leopold di Köthen, per ridurre al minimo il numero e il costo dei musicisti coinvolti nei viaggi.

Ultima osservazione: il carattere meditativo ed errabondo di molti dei pezzi per Violino e Violoncello che abbiamo in mente oggigiorno è una eredità deformante delle interpretazioni tardo romantiche dei secoli scorsi, che consideravano queste Suites come musica pura da salotto, slegata da danze, o come meri esercizi tecnici (!). Negli ultimi decenni diversi interpreti hanno mostrato quanto le danze delle Suites per Violoncello possano essere suonate pienamente come danze, con il loro carattere ritmico originale. Le Suites per Clavicembalo hanno subito meno questa *dislettura* romantica.

2.2 Disvelamento dei segreti della 2a Suite "a Violoncello Solo senza basso"

2.2.1 Il Preludio della seconda Suite

Nel 1984, da liceale, mi capitò di suonare le Suites per Violoncello solo in una sala con pareti di legno (una piccola cappella nelle Alpi francesi, abbastanza riverberante e con eco) e rimasi impressionato da uno strano effetto sonoro: mentre suonavo avevo l'impressione di accompagnarmi da solo. Mi ripromisi di approfondire la cosa.

Nell'estate del 1991, suonando il Preludio della 2ª Suite, ascoltando attentamente e cantando l'inizio di questo pezzo melodico mi accorsi che funzionava a canone. Dopo una breve analisi scritta mi accorsi che tutto il Preludio funzionava come canone. Su questa traccia sviluppai (malamente) gli accordi finali in modo che la melodia continuasse in canone e stampai il pezzo come duo da suonare a due violoncelli o con violino (all'ottava) e violoncello. Qualche anno dopo testandolo con un amico, osservò che alcune parti non funzionavano bene, così mi ripromisi di sistemarle appena possibile. Nel 2019 (!) finalmente ripresi il pezzo su un computer con un nuovo software di base e vidi che in effetti c'erano diverse battute problematiche. Ci misi un po' a proporre una soluzione a canone, perché questo necessitava di trasformare completamente la melodia. Accessoriamente cominciai a chiedermi perché Bach non avesse composto queste battute a canone come il resto del pezzo. Non riuscendo a trovare

Figura 3: 2a Suite, canone a due voci

una risposta ripresi l'analisi del pezzo e visivamente vidi che c'era spazio per una terza voce in canone: provai subito e funzionava! Spiegherò più tardi perché avevo appena messo piede in un mondo molto più complesso, adesso ci voleva molto più tempo e fatica per trovare una soluzione alle battute problematiche e anche lo sviluppo degli accordi finali andava ritoccato. In più qualunque soluzione trovassi (non è un problema a soluzione unica) risultava insoddisfacente musicalmente rispetto al resto dell'originale di Bach. Infine per il canone a tre voci fu necessario correggere anche qualche nota sporadica nel resto del pezzo, devastandone abbastanza la linearità melodica. Anche più recentemente nel 2023 ho provato a trovare soluzioni migliori (specialmente per lo sviluppo degli accordi finali), ma la serie di battute problematiche resistono ancora: restano un bell'esercizio se volete cimentarvi!

La mia spiegazione di perché questa sezione del pezzo originale (identica nelle versioni di Anna Magdalena e di Kellner) non funzionasse a canone fu che J.S. Bach aveva composto la Suite appena dopo la morte improvvisa della moglie e che aveva lasciato un "buco" in corrispondenza delle sezioni e della fine del pezzo, con qualche indicazione di accordi, da "completare in seguito". Probabilmente non trovò mai la forza d'animo di completare questo pezzo perché l'associava dolorosamente al lutto e il pezzo fu completato e corretto dall'estrosa ed elegante Anna Magdalena Wilcke. Un'altra possibile versione è che nessuno comprendeva perché ci mettesse così tanto a finire un semplice pezzo per Violoncello solo e che abbia dovuto chiuderlo in fretta tra un impegno e l'altro per venderlo, ma non credo, perché le Suites furono dapprima date al suo alunno Kellner e pubblicate solo molti anni dopo. Forse le doveva dare a Kellner, o ad un altro violoncellista in occasione di un ballo di corte, in ogni caso il probabile intento originale di essere un regalo per il Principe Leopold, che suonava la Viola da Gamba, era svanito, perché il Principe non era un grande musicista e le Suites non erano facilissime da suonare, quindi non c'era fretta di completare la "confezione regalo".

2.2.2 Gli accordi finali non sviluppati

A seguito di questa scoperta, la vecchia diatriba tra violoncellisti sul dover o meno sviluppare gli accordi finali del Preludio della 2a Suite direi che è risolta: con l'intervallo di tempo breve tra le diverse voci, si potrebbe anche accettare una versione accorciata degli accordi, come nelle Figura 5, per evitare di accavallarli, ma sono convinto che vadano sviluppati per completare il triplo canone in modo melodico e discorsivo, come nell'esempio della Figura 6.

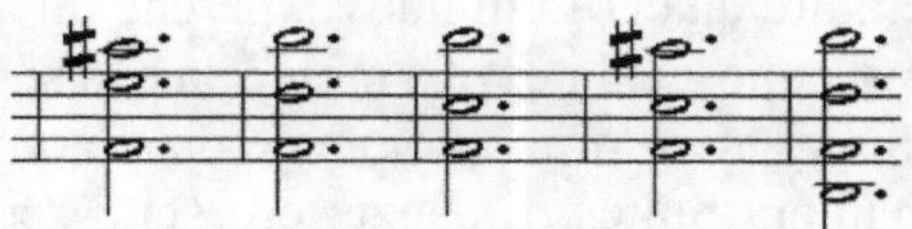

Figura 4: accordi nello spartito originale

Figura 5: accordi accettabili nel triplo canone

Figura 6: esempio di sviluppo in canone a tre voci degli accordi

2.2.3 Disvelamento del resto della seconda Suite per violoncello

A questo punto pensavo che questa scoperta di un canone a tre voci nascosto in un pezzo così bello e lungo come il Preludio fosse un notevole unicum nella storia della musica, ma così per gioco provai ad estendere l'analisi al secondo pezzo della Suite, l'Allemanda: incredibilmente era anche lei un doppio canone, a questo punto mi toccava vedere tutte le danze, una per una, la Corrente, la Sarabanda, la coppia di Minuetti e la Giga svelarono i loro tesori. Mi toccava ricopiare lo spartito nota per nota, usando il poco tempo dei fine settimana fine 2021 per fortuna nelle danze non ci furono i problemi che avevo avuto con il Preludio, solo qualche nota spuria da "correggere", ma ad ogni triplo canone scoperto corrispondeva una grande gioia e il piacere di ascoltare qualcosa di nuovo, perché, incredibilmente, anche quando si conosce il pezzo a memoria e lo si assembla non si riesce ad immaginare prima come suona il contro-canone, e questo per un'intera Suites di danze: ero stato seduto per anni sopra la cassa del tesoro senza accorgermene!

Per finire ho condiviso gli spartiti in un paio di siti web (IMSLP and AIMA music) e ho presentato la scoperta in un webinar.

2.3 *I segreti delle altre cinque Suites per Violoncello*

Nei mesi successivi del 2022 ho esteso la ricerca alle altre Suites per violoncello, scoprendo la stessa struttura nascosta di canone a tre voci, anche nell'insospettabile Preludio e fuga della quinta Suite che ha la doppia struttura di contro-canone e fuga: un capolavoro assoluto! L'ultimo pezzo dell'ultima Suite, una Giga, funziona addirittura come canone a 10 voci! L'ho adattato e semplificato un po' per insieme di fiati (per distinguere meglio i timbri di ogni voce).

E' interessante notare come alcuni passaggi o note singole non soddisfino il canone a tre voci, per esempio nel Preludio della prima Suite: forse Bach ha lasciato un "buco" da completare in seguito, o un incidente ha cancellato lo spartito (acqua sull'inchiostro, topo rosicchiatore ?) e qualcuno (Anna

Magdalena ?) ha trovato una melodia ragionevole per completare il tutto.

Il modo di far funzionare il canone è molto vario e questo ha reso questa ricerca un viaggio pieno di sorprese, con il premio di ascoltare gli effetti nascosti. Inoltre ho osservato che in ogni Suite c'era un unico pezzo che funzionava addirittura come canone a 7 voci (se si tollerano le 4e e le 5e parallele), senza perdere subito la chiarezza della struttura, un pezzo diverso per ognuna delle sei Suites, che prelevato e messo con le altre eccezioni formava una "settima Suite per 7 violoncelli".

Un ricercatore [6b] ha proposto di attribuire tutte le Suites per Violoncello alla moglie di Bach, ma direi che dopo questa ricerca (soprattutto per i paragrafi che seguono) posso affermare che l'ascolto interno dei canoni a tre (o più) voci è come una firma di J.S. Bach che nessuno può imitare. Spiegherò perché nella seconda parte del libricino.

Negli allegati ho messo l'indirizzo alla guida dei canoni delle Suites per violoncello (con l'inizio di ogni pezzo e l'intervallo tra le voci) e ho messo in rete degli audio per dare un assaggio dei canoni.

2.4 Scoperta delle Suites per altri strumenti solisti

Dopo aver analizzato 6x7 = 42 pezzi nelle Suites per violoncello, mi era ormai chiaro che J.S. Bach era un "canonatore seriale": aveva un modo naturale e spontaneo di ascoltare e comporre melodie che nascondevano dei canoni, come una malattia professionale (ce ne fossero tante di così!) per qualche ragione misteriosa che dovevo chiarire.

Per verificarlo dovevo ispezionare più pezzi. Con in mente la tesi dei "kit da viaggio" per il Principe Leopold, nel primo quadrimestre del 2022 ho esteso l'analisi alle altre opere composte da Bach nella sua corte per strumenti soli melodici: le Suites per Violino e quella per Flauto traverso.

Tenete a mente che quando dico "analizzare un pezzo" in realtà significa copiare lo spartito pazientemente nota per nota sul computer in modo analogo a quanto faceva Bach stesso su carta quando era ragazzo e scopriva i capolavori dei suoi contemporanei, solo senza il suo stress di non dover commettere errori, di non fare macchie di inchiostro, di non rompere le piume e di non sprecare carta ed essere punito per questo! Il secondo passo è più facile di questo lavoro da amanuense: un semplice copia e incolla della prima voce su altre portate cercando lo sfasamento giusto per ottenere almeno un 80% di sovrapposizione gradevole e sensata formalmente. Ci sono modi più comodi di fare questo lavoro (purtroppo ci ho pensato dopo!) nei nostri tempi moderni: basta trovare un file già trascritto su siti come musescore, o trovare un file in formato midi e importarlo nei programmi di videoscrittura musicale, roba di disk jokey. È molto più veloce ma si impara molto meno e soprattutto partendo dai files audio, la trascrizione può essere molto sbagliata ritmicamente rispetto all'originale e lo spartito risulta completamente sbagliato. Inoltre vi perdete il piacere di leggere gli spartiti originali scritti a mano da Bach e dalla sua famiglia/ditta, con i segni di commento, le linee eleganti che già suggeriscono l'interpretazione: una musica per gli occhi, e tutto il piacere di trovare errori o discrepanze tra diverse versioni, insomma manca tutto il gusto della Storia!

Per fare in fretta (nelle Suites per Violino ci sono tantissime note da copiare rispetto a quelle per Violoncello) e con un certo azzardo, basato sulla mia ipotesi numerologica, che esporrò in un paragrafo apposito, mi focalizzai direttamente sulla ricerca dei "pezzi speciali" delle sei Sonate e Partite (BWV 1001-1006) che funzionavano come canoni a 7 voci, sperando che ce ne fossero, uno diverso per ogni Suite come in quelle per violoncello. Cominciai dai mei pezzi preferiti e vidi che funzionavano bene, quindi mi fermai lì, mi limitai a sette pezzi, che di nuovo chiamai "settima Suite nascosta per violino solo".

Per gli amici musicologi che vogliono proseguire il lavoro, gli altri pezzi per violino sono a vostra disposizione per svelare i loro contro-canoni ed ascoltarli dopo trecento anni: vi assicuro che ne vale la pena e che è tempo speso bene!

Fatto questo restava solo la Partita BWV 1013 per Flauto traverso: la Allemanda, la Corrente, la Sarabande, la Bourrée Anglaise rivelarono I loro canoni nascosti a quattro voci. Per "completare" questa sfortunata Suite incompleta, che sembra incompiuta, diedi un'occhiata ad altri pezzi famosi di Bach per Flauto solo o accompagnato: mancava un *Preludio*, identificato con la BWV 846 e aggiunsi come pezzo finale la *Badinerie* BWV 1067, svelando I loro canoni nascosti. Probabilmente Bach aveva riutilizzato il materiale per Flauto solo della Suite completa per fare opere più elaborate e di successo. Devo ammettere che il risultato sonoro e musicale della Suite per Flauto a canone multiplo è molto meno soddisfacente e convincente di quello delle Suites per Violino o Violoncello. Questo può spiegare perché Bach si sia sentito libero di smembrare la Suite e lasciarne solo le spoglie nella BWV 1013. Per arricchire ulteriormente la Suite per Flauto, ho analizzato recentemente la *Gigue* dalla Suite per Liuto BWV 997, che funziona come canone a 5 voci, e il famoso *Siciliano* dalla Sonata BWV 1031 che funziona come canone a 7 voci.

A questo punto avevo finito le Suite per strumenti melodici, a voce singola che poteva necessitare di un accompagnamento immanente. Ma ascoltando le Suite per tastiera, le Suite Francesi (BWV 812-817) e le Suite Inglesi (BWV 806-811) mi saltò all'orecchio che la densità di note non era molto alta considerando le dieci dita a disposizione: benché perfette erano piuttosto rarefatte. Così nelle vacanze estive del 2022 analizzai tutti gli inizi di tutti i pezzi delle Suites trovando la struttura nascosta di canone a tre voci: tutte queste Suites possono essere suonate da tre clavicembali o pianoforti. Anche qui "completai" le Suites Francesi con I Preludi mancanti, pescati da quelli "di scorta" preparati da Bach, abbinandoli per tonalità, (BWV 935, BWV 934, BWV 925, BWV 876, BWV 816, BWV 937).

L'analisi di queste Suite per clavicembalo mi stava dicendo parecchie cose, perché non erano state scritte nel periodo di Köthen per il Principe Leopold, ma precedentemente. Di conseguenza la mia ipotesi del "Suite da viaggio per Leopold" non era per forza giusta! In ogni modo bisogna osservare che degli spartiti per un solo musicista capaci di animare una festa da ballo restavano commercialmente una grande idea, e che quelle per Clavicembalo potevano servire a Bach stesso per eventuali trasferte. Penso che le prime Suites composte siano state quelle Francesi, per I motivi esposti nel paragrafo delle influenze, senza I Preludi, con l'idea di pescarne uno diverso ogni volta, o di improvvisarlo, prima di suonare le danze, per questo troviamo molti Preludi separati e sfusi, in molte tonalità e atmosfere, per ogni occasione.

2.5 Conseguenze su come suonare le Suites di Bach

A dire il vero dopo queste scoperte penso che un musicista possa tranquillamente continuare a suonare le Suites da solo nelle solite sale da concerto, perché Bach non ha esplicitato I suoi canoni multipli. Ma adesso si possono suonare anche in gruppo, oppure con l'ausilio di un sistema audio che aggiunge eco artificiali, o mettendosi in ambienti ricchi di eco ed *adattando il tempo di esecuzione alla sala* (come mi era successo nel 1984) per far scoprire ad un pubblico maggiore le meraviglie dei canoni multipli.

Per quanto riguarda l'interpretazione delle Suite I musicisti possono continuare a fare le loro romanticherie e le versioni manieristiche estreme, ma devono sapere che adesso è sicuro che *Bach non le ascoltava così*. La presenza di due voci supplementari è totalmente incompatibile con variazioni improvvise di tempo e con respiri eccessivi tra due frasi, abusati dai sospiranti romantici. Siate sicuri che *evitare pause ed adottare un tempo di esecuzione stabile, o con piccole variazioni progressive (accelerazioni e decelerazioni)* è più consono all'intento originale e alla presenza dei canoni immanenti.

Devo infine sottolineare che suonare le Suites in canone, con più strumenti, è un esercizio musicale eccellente, perché richiede un controllo preciso della velocità, al quale non siamo abituati suonandole da soli, e un controllo perfetto dell'intensità sonora delle diverse voci, perché le melodie diventano anche accompagnamento: il mio suggerimento è di eseguire sempre la prima voce più forte e di fare le altre man mano più deboli, così come succede con le eco naturali.

2.6 *Excursus eccentrico sulla numerologia*

Qui devo spendere qualche parola sulla numerologia nelle Suites di Bach. È un argomento frivolo ma che meriterebbe approfondimenti. Al tempo di J.S. Bach la numerologia era una conoscenza importante e pervasiva, che ognuno usava, più o meno, nolente o volente, per costruire le sue abitudini mentali e le sue credenze, come le superstizioni, basandosi su esperienze personali o su regole e convenzioni collettive.

Dando un'occhiata alla lista completa delle Suites composte da J.S. Bach (per esempio su https://en.wikipedia.org/wiki/Suite_(Bach), o nell'archivio ufficiale di Leipzig), osserviamo immediatamente che è composta da alcuni **set** completi di 6 Suite: **un** gruppo per Violoncello (BWV 1007-1012), **uno** per Violino (BWV 1001-1006), **quattro** per Clavicembalo (BWV 806-811, BWV 812-817, BWV 825-830, BWV 818-824). In ogni Suite ci sono tipicamente **sei** danze. Così vedete bene che se i set fossero sei si otterrebbe il "numero satanico" 666, cosa assolutamente inaccettabile per un campione della musica considerata come suprema espressione religiosa cf [9b], fortunatamente c'è qualche Suite in più: le Suite e Ouverture per Clavicembalo

(BWV 831, BWV 832-845), o Liuto (BWV 995-998), o Orchestra (BWV1066-1069-1070?), senza parlare dei movimenti "di scorta" (prevalentemente Preludi). A maggiore smentita aggiungo che il raggruppamento in set è stato fatto dopo la morte di Bach, così non c'è nessun motivo per supporre intenti satanici da parte di Bach e potete anche dimenticarvi di questo paragrafo.

Ma su questo tema numerologico dobbiamo ricordarci che J.S. Bach era il 7º figlio di 7 figli di una splendida famiglia che costruì un paradiso musicale attorno a lui, per sette anni, prima di collassare. Inoltre la sua educazione musicale ha avuto luogo nella chiesa di San Michele a Ohrdruf e nella Scuola di San Michele a Lüneburg. Ora San Michele è l'angelo incaricato di suonare la prima delle **sette** trombe dell'Apocalisse. Ne consegue che Bach deve aver avuto una relazione positiva col numero sette, senza contare che nella cultura occidentale il numero sette è considerato generalmente un numero fortunato, associato al settimo giorno, quello del riposo, e che rappresenta così il *completamento del ciclo della creazione* (nella Bibbia) e la settimana santa della Passione cristiana musicata più volte da Bach, mentre il numero 6 rappresenta una creazione incompleta ed inaccettabile. Questo può spiegare perché nelle Suites per Violoncello e in molte altre Bach abbia inserito il Preludio (e lo componesse dopo) come settimo movimento, a coronamento delle sei danze, sull'esempio di Marin Marais (meno preciso col numero di danze). Inoltre a completamento delle Suites Francesi si sono i Preludi di scorta I Preludi e Fuga, inclusi quelli del Clavicembalo ben temperato. Come detto in precedenza il Preludio non era solo una composizione che preparava una particolare atmosfera e stile al tempo ludico delle danze, ma anche una forma di intrattenimento più virtuoso ed estroso da ascoltare. In ogni caso la "settima Suite nascosta" per Violoncello e quella per Violino le ho proposte in questa logica numerologica di completamento simbolico e di necessità di evitare le sei 6 Suites di sei pezzi. Riguardo ai quattro set di Suite per Clavicembalo, penso che non ci sia bisogno di cercare ulteriori caratteristiche complesse in alcuni pezzi per fabbricare la settima Suite perché ci sono già molte Suite spurie al di fuori dei raggruppamenti istituiti.

2.7 *Estensione dell'analisi ad altri capolavori*

Dalla lista delle Suites e dalle osservazioni sopra riportate, molti altri canoni multipli sono ancora nascosti e scopribili dai lettori scettici, tanto nelle Partite e Sonate quanto nelle Suites per Clavicembalo, o per Liuto: provare per credere. Me le sono lasciate per una eventuale pensione!

Per capire se i canoni multipli nascosti fossero una costante sistematica di J.S. Bach, non limitata alle Suites, mi lanciai nell'analisi di qualche Concerto. Ho scoperto che:

1) nel Concerto per Violino BWV 1041, la parte di Violino solo nasconde un canone a tre voci, cioè può essere suonata con tre solisti!

2) nel Concerto per due Violini BWV 1043 entrambi I Violini solisti nascondono canoni a quattro voci, cioè il pezzo può essere suonato con otto solisti!

3) Nel Concerto per Oboe e Violino BWV 1060R ognuna delle due voci solistiche nasconde un canone a quattro voci, cioè può essere suonato con 8 solisti, 4 Violini e 4 Oboi! In più anche le quattro corde dell'orchestra nel primo movimento potrebbero funzionare in canone a quattro voci, sicché quattro orchestre possono suonare contemporaneamente il pezzo...

4) nell'Allegro del 5° Brandenburghese, le parti di Flauto solo e Violino solo sono compatibili con dei canoni a quattro voci, cioè il pezzo si può suonare con 4 Violini e 4 solo Flauti.

5) Non sono riuscito a trovare canoni nascosti funzionanti negli altri movimenti del 5° Brandeburghese, questo significa che

a) forse J.S. Bach non usava I canoni nascosti se non aveva tempo o voglia, oppure delegava a sua moglie o ai suoi figli/e il compito di completare I pezzi della ditta Bach, senza richiedere i canoni nascosti.

b) in ogni caso la composizione contrappuntistica da sola non implica la possibilità di trovare canoni multipli nascosti!

Tutte gli spartiti frutto di queste ricerche sono liberamente disponibili sui sisti IMSLP (vedere le sezioni "arrangiamenti" e "altro") e AIMAmusic (<u>https://aimamusic.it/nuova-musica/</u>).

2.8 Obiezioni contrappuntistiche

Alcuni musicisti mi hanno detto che trovare canoni è un'ovvietà in una composizione contrappuntistica: questa osservazione vale (e non sempre) per dei canoni a due voci, o per semplici melodie con un andamento oscillante e ripetuto in cicli regolari, come quello esemplificato da Bach nel canone BWV 1072, ma diventa totalmente falsa quando si tratta di canoni a tre voci e di melodie complesse come quelle delle Suite: basta che alcune battute cambino in un modo incompatibile con quello delle battute precedenti, come le battute problematiche della seconda Suite per violoncello, o quelle degli altri movimenti del 5° Brandeburghese, pur conservando uno stile contrappuntistico. Se non siete convinti provate a comporre un canone a tre voci e capirete, oppure cercate canoni nascosti in altri autori di pezzi contrappuntistici!

Il capitolo seguente fornisce ulteriori chiarimenti sulla complessità dei canoni multipli di Bach, e non sono quelli risaputi, basati sulla guida/testamento BWV 1087.

3 La difficoltà di comporre canoni multipli

3.1 Cos'è un canone?

Il canone, nel senso musicale, è un modo interessante di accompagnare una melodia usando come seconda voce la stessa melodia ritardata nel tempo. Da un punto di vista simbolico il canone rappresenta le diverse generazioni che coesistono in momenti diversi della loro esistenza nascendo e morendo in momenti scalati nel tempo, una dopo l'altra. Il canone è spesso usato in forme cicliche infinite, ricominciando la melodia appena finisce e dando forma sonora al "panta rei" degli antichi Greci, con la storia che si ripete all'infinito, o alla metempsicosi induista.

Dal punto di vista pratico della composizione ogni elemento della melodia composta, per funzionare come canone, deve potersi sovrapporre tanto con l'elemento successivo che con quello precedente. La lunghezza dell'"elemento" corrisponde al ritardo nel tempo tra le voci.

Nelle canzoni popolari si trova spesso una forma semplificata del canone, nella quale gli elementi della melodia si ripetono, o si alternano, identici a sé stessi, in modo che bastino solo due elementi compatibili uno con l'altro.

La rappresentazione grafica di questi **"canoni triviali"** può essere fatta usando un colore per ogni elemento della melodia, disegnandoli sulla linea del tempo che scorre:

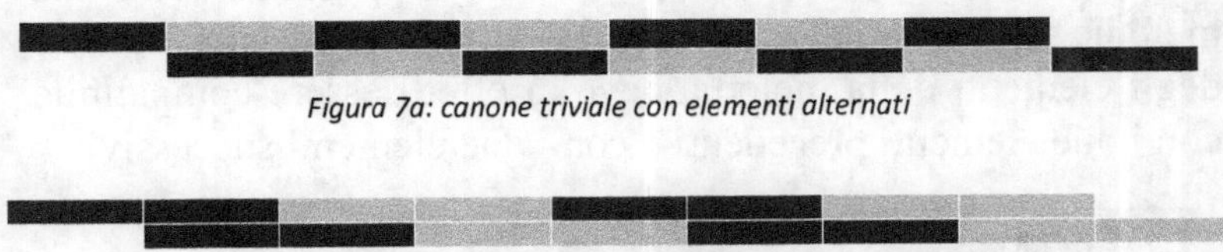

Figura 7a: canone triviale con elementi alternati

Figura 7b: canone triviale con elementi ripetuti

Si può osservare che questi canoni triviali funzionano anche aggiungendo ulteriori voci, ma nel caso degli elementi alternati della figura 7a, la terza voce è identica alla prima, mentre nel caso di elementi ripetuti della Figura 7b la quinta voce è identica alla prima. In entrambi I casi gli elementi sovrapposti sono sempre gli stessi e questo tipo di musica è stucchevole ed utilizzata per canti da bambini, che amano le attività ripetute ossessivamente. Ciò nonostante l'effetto di sovrapporre una melodia scalata con se stessa crea di per sé una nuova sensazione, un piacere sui generis ed un nuovo elemento complessivo: è l'elemento di base della *metamusica* (cf [11]).

Si possono poi trovare **"canoni evolutivi"**, nei quali gli elementi che si susseguono cambiano continuamente, non si ripetono mai. In questa forma ogni elemento deve essere gradevolmente compatibile contemporaneamente con l'elemento successivo e con quello precedente, che non sono identici come nel canone triviale. La rappresentazione grafica diventa la seguente:

Figura 8: canone evolutivo semplice con elementi sempre diversi

Questo canone è più interessante e "difficile" da comporre ed evita ripetizioni stucchevoli.

3.2 I canoni multipli

A partire dalla terza voce ("doppio canone" o "contro-canone") la complessità aumenta drasticamente e quasi nessuno riesce a sentire in anticipo che effetto avrà la sovrapposizione e se una melodia saprà soddisfare i requisiti del canone a tre voci: ognuno degli elementi della melodia deve in effetti essere compatibile con i due elementi precedenti e con i due elementi successivi:

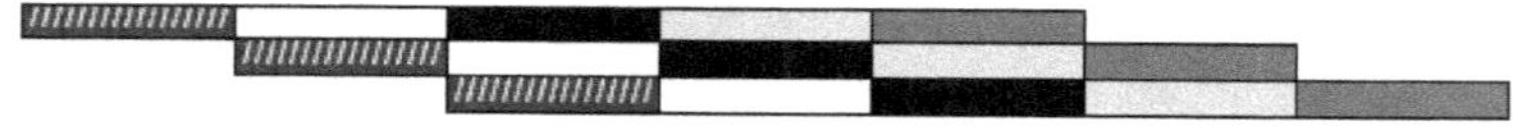

Figura 9: doppio canone evolutivo (a 3 voci)

Più aumenta il numero delle voci da sovrapporre in un canone evolutivo, più aumenta la complessità del comporre ogni elemento e quella dell'ascolto: per n voci ogni elemento deve essere compatibile con 2 x (n-1) elementi. Per esempio, per 5 voci ogni elemento deve essere compatibile con 8 elementi (4 prima e 4 dopo), come mostrato nello schema seguente:

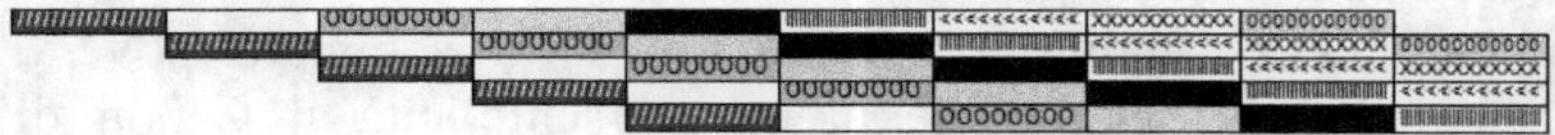

Figure 10: canone evolutivo a 5 voci

Adesso potete capire un po' meglio perché ero in difficoltà con le battute mancanti del Preludio della seconda Suite e potete anche capire che realizzare il canone ad otto voci della Figura 1 non è semplicissimo, tanto meno se deve anche essere piacevole, anche con l'ausilio di un computer: pensate ora ai canoni a sette voci delle Suites e a quello a dieci voci della Giga dell'ultima per Violoncello. La presenza di canoni multipli nascosti, immanenti, spiega pienamente la particolare forma contorta e lo stile particolare delle melodie di Bach, che si può osservare confrontandole con quelle di altri autori e che mi ha sempre intrigato prima di questa scoperta.

3.3   *Contesto canonico all'epoca di J.S. Bach*

Per avere un'informazione più completa, vi invito a riferirvi ai lavori di Denis Collins [1] e [4]. Lasciatemi solo fare un paio di osservazioni. Considerando il modesto contesto di J.S. Bach durante gli anni passati a Ohrdruf ospitato da suo fratellone organista Johann Christoph, con pochi (costosi) spartiti da copiare, forse di nascosto, o da imparare a memoria, sembra poco probabile che J.S.B. possa aver scoperto i *Ricercari, canone e sonate per 2 violoncelli* (1689) di Domenico Gabrielli, che erano canoni evolutivi in una forma semplificata, che alterna tratti di melodia ad una voce con tratti di accompagnamento

 119

mentre la melodia passa alla seconda voce. Al contrario sembra sicuro che nel contesto germanico Bach conoscesse il famoso *Canone e Giga in Re maggiore*, (1680, P.37) di Johann Pachelbel, che era stato l'insegnate di suo fratello: questo pezzo ha una linea di basso ostinato e tre voci in forma di canone evolutivo semplificata, con alternanza di frasi e accompagnamenti, gli elementi sono lunghi, ma rimangono nella stessa tonalità e l'armonia è tutto sommato povera. Malgrado, o forse grazie a, questa semplicità il Canon di Pachelbel è tutt'ora un successo mondiale e fu senz'altro una scoperta ed un riferimento per il giovane Bach.

3.4 *I canoni evolutivi e modulanti di Bach*

Entrambi i pezzi citati però restano nella stessa tonalità dall'inizio alla fine. Al contrario I canoni evolutivi di Bach richiedono un livello più alto di compatibilità tra elementi adiacenti, perché possono essere in tonalità diverse (melodia modulante). I canoni a tre voci evolutivi sono già difficili da comporre in una sola tonalità, ma richiedono il talento di un genio per essere modulanti e conservare melodie bellissime. Probabilmente Bach ha imparato come cambiare facilmente tonalità in occasione della sua avventura a Lubecca, con un viaggio a piedi di 400 km per spiare il famoso organista-improvvisatore Dieterich Buxtehude col suo stylus phantasticus e Preludi e Fughe.

Certamente i canoni-gambero, o quelli riflessi, o quelli "per augmentationem o diminutionem" delle BWV 1087 sono ancora più complessi dal punto di vista teorico, ma d'altro canto sono meno udibili e poco godibili senza un supporto visivo. In ogni caso lo studio di questo libricino si concentra su canoni udibili, modulanti, multipli, nascosti.

4 Commenti sulle "Guide ai canoni" allegate

4.1 Le guide brevi ai canoni

Negli spartiti indicati negli allegati potrete trovare tutti gli inizi dei vari pezzi con i vari ritardi tra le voci in canone per le Suite Francesi "completate" e per quelle Inglesi e anche per i vari Concerti che ho esplorato. Il fatto di indicare solo l'inizio dei pezzi, oltre a risparmiare carta, permette ai musicisti di continuare ad utilizzare la loro edizione abituale e di applicare solo il ritardo nell'esecuzione con altri musicisti. Le Suites per Violoncello sono invece riportate interamente perché ho avuto la pessima idea di "correggerle", come ho spiegato in precedenza, cosa che non rifarei, perché la scoperta dei canoni nascosti è l'interesse principale di questo lavoro e perché le varianti proposte nelle melodie per essere più compatibili con i canoni multipli sono sempre meno belle dell'originale, anche nei casi in cui mancavano dei pezzi (fine della sesta Suite), o erano visibilmente rattoppi (seconda Suite per Violoncello) ed occorrerebbe un lavoro di "restauro conservativo", per musicologi pazienti. Anche alcuni pezzi particolari delle Suites per Violino, la Suite per Flauto "completata", e gli arrangiamenti per trio d'archi (violino-viola-violoncello), o per fanfara di strumenti a fiato, sono riportati con spartiti completi per permettere un'esecuzione più agevole. Sono tutti sui Siti web IMSLP e AIMAmusic.

4.2 I sorprendenti ritmi sincopici nascosti

La complessità ritmica che si può osservare in alcuni pezzi il lato più sorprendente e controverso di questi canoni nascosti a tre voci. Dal punto di vista di potenziali detrattori potrebbe essere descritto come un trucco triviale per sfuggire agli accordi dissonanti, perché le note sono scalate nel tempo più finemente e questo può sembrare un espediente poco consono all'epoca di Bach. Ma avendo cercato soluzioni per parecchio tempo posso assicurare che questo "trucco" non funziona per tutti i pezzi, quando non si trova nessun canone decente, crea soltanto confusione. Per di più la stessa complessità ritmica dei controtempi può essere riscontrata negli archetipi pedagogici proposti da Bach nella guida BWV 1072. La conseguenza di questo è che questo ritmo immanente, tipico di più tarde rapsodie romantiche e dei Ragtimes del novecento, l'ha scoperto Bach e probabilmente non l'ha palesato perché risultava troppo moderno per il suo tempo e certamente troppo destabilizzante per delle danze di corte, molto lontane dai locali da ballo moderni.

4.3 L'atmosfera da chiesa nell'ascolto dei canoni multipli

Fatta eccezione per i pezzi citati precedentemente con effetti ritmici divertenti, gli altri pezzi a canone analizzati creano una atmosfera e una sonorità di musica da chiesa, piena di eco e risonanze. Ascoltati per un tempo troppo lungo, a causa dell'attenzione e della concentrazione che richiede la loro complessità risultano affaticanti. Anche questo spiega perché Bach non abbia proposto le versioni a canone multiplo esplicito di questi pezzi, da suonare con più strumenti, malgrado il guadagno superiore che ne avrebbe ottenuto (gli spartiti erano pagati proporzionalmente alla loro lunghezza e numero di note!): sarebbero stati molto meno apprezzati delle versioni per un solo strumento. Perché allora fare tanta fatica nel comporre canoni multipli tenendoli nascosti? La seconda parte del libro si cimenta nel rispondere a questo interrogativo.

PARTE II FATTI NON FUMMO A VIVER COME BRUTI

5 La necessità è la madre di tutte le virtù

È tempo ora di provare a capire perché J.S. Bach componesse in questo modo così particolare e perché ne fosse così fiero da far

Fig. 11 Johann Sebastian Bach (aged 61) nel ritratto di Elias Gottlob Haussmann, seconda versione del canevaccio del 1746. Bach impugna il suo canone a sei voci BWV 1076 e ce lo porge.
http://www.jsbach.net/bass/elements/bach-haussmann.jpg ,
https://commons.wikimedia.org/w/index.php?curid=1270015

figurare nel suo ritratto-testamento dei canoni multipli come summa del lavoro di una vita.

Anche il suo Monogramma (sigillo) ha una corona al centro: era conscio di essere (e sarà per sempre) il Re dei canoni. Un'osservazione più precisa rivela delle serie di tre linee parallele, che possono richiamare i canoni a tre voci, rispecchiate, per richiamare forse quelli inversi ("a gambero"), ancora da scoprire da qualche parte …

Fig.12 Sigillo di Bach, usato nei suoi anni di Lipsia. Contiene al centro le sue iniziali J S B specchiate e incoronate. Sui fianchi le lettere sono spacchettate.

https://commons.wikimedia.org/wiki/File:Bach_Seal.svg#filelinks

5.1 La straordinaria vita di J.S. Bach

Nessuno di un talento che ha dalla nascita può essere fiero, ma se lo ha sviluppato con duro esercizio e dura vita, allora lo può essere invero.

Johann Sebastian era l'ultimo di sette figli e fu sicuramente coccolato da genitori, fratelli sorelle e istruito anche da altri zii musicisti giocava e suonava su tanti strumenti diversi, dal violino al clavicembalo e cresceva spensierato in un piccolo borgo del Sacro Romano Impero di Occidente. Aveva solo nove anni quando sua madre morì, suo padre non fu capace di sopravviverle molti mesi e la famiglia collassò. Il paradiso infantile era perso per sempre. Il suo fratello maggiore per fortuna aveva già un lavoro da organista nella chiesa di San

Michele di Ohrdruf e lo ospitò insieme ad un altro fratellino. La scuola certo non offriva protezione (cf [13]). Possiamo solo immaginare che in questa nuova vita J.S. trovò rifugio nella chiesa, imparando a suonare l'organo da suo fratello, per gioco e per diventare a sua volta un musicista. Sicuramente imparava a memoria e quando poteva copiava tutti i preziosi spartiti in circolazione, a rischio di farsi punire per lo spreco della preziosa carta, per scoprire la musica dei compositori del sud della Germania, suonandoli e capendo come componevano. Era intelligente e brillante, tanto da essere selezionato per una borsa di studio nella famosa Scuola di San Michele di Lüneburg. L'importante per quanto ci riguarda è che passò sicuramente un sacco di tempo suonando l'organo della chiesa, superando in questo modo ogni tendenza autistica causata dal trauma dell'essere rimasto orfano, perché divenne un campione di improvvisazione.

5.2 L'acustica architettonica come contesto scatenante

Nel mondo di J.S. Bach, la musica era suonata nei Templi Luterani, spogli ed austeri, o nelle sale vuote con pareti di pietra dei palazzi, al massimo arricchite da qualche arazzo. Da un punto di vista acustico, entrambe queste tipologie di spazio erano caratterizzate da un tempo di riverberazione lungo e da qualche eco dominante. Nelle chiese chiamate Hallenkirchen, col soffitto di medesima altezza nella navata centrale e nelle navate laterali, le due eco principali corrispondevano una alla lunghezza della navata e l'altra all'altezza costante della chiesa. Ne risultava certamente un certo caos acustico e un ascolto molto difficile della musica e dei discorsi, specie a distanze maggiori di due o tre metri dai musicisti, o dagli oratori. Degli spazi migliori acusticamente potevano essere i chiostri, i cortili e le pubbliche piazze, ma il clima tedesco ne limitava l'utilizzo alla stagione calda, o agli strumenti a fiato, meno sensibili alle variazioni di temperatura e umidità rispetto agli strumenti che usavano corde di budello. L'altra alternativa valida acusticamente erano le taverne affollate, ma erano posti da menestrelli e musicanti che nessun compositore avrebbe preso in considerazione (anche perché non avrebbe condiviso i guadagni dei suonatori). Nelle chiese cattoliche barocche, grazie alla varietà di forme, cappellette, nicchie, statue, colonne e innumerevoli ornamenti di stucco, pannelli di legno, che agivano come diffusori naturali, la presenza delle eco era mitigata e un genio come Bach non avrebbe avuto l'occasione di risolvere questo problema. Idem oggi con i pannelli fonoassorbenti. Fatto sta che per il giovane Bach che passava il suo tempo sull'organo della chiesa di Ohrdruf (una Hallenkirche), il maggiore problema acustico era di ottenere una musica chiara e nitida, lottando contro le risonanze e rombi onnipresenti, le sovrapposizioni disarmoniche, il disordine sonoro, questa confusione che era inaccettabile ed incompatibile con il concetto di ordine e armonia, fondamentale per la sua Religione, per la filosofia Leibniziana che permeava la sua formazione.

5.3 *La geniale soluzione di Bach*

Dopo aver rinvenuto così tanti canoni a tre voci sono arrivato alla **tesi** che la soluzione geniale che elaborò il giovane Bach per far fronte al problema acustico delle eco nelle sale dove suonava fu di *adattare la musica*, in modo da *ottenere una sovrapposizione armoniosa con le eco*, una specie di sinergia con il suono emesso dagli strumenti, per *emergere dalla confusione del campo diffuso e riverberante*, che costituiva un rumore di fondo incoerente da sconfiggere.

Per arrivare a questa scoperta **due eccezionali doni** erano necessari. Il primo, un grande talento di adattare la propria esecuzione agli eventi sonori esterni, anche chiamata *improvvisazione allenata,* l'intenso desiderio di novità e l'abilità di improvvisare liberamente, gli fu *regalato dalla noia,* una volta esplorati, sfruttati ed esauriti gli spartiti di suo fratello. Il secondo, uno *sviluppo di capacità uditive fuori dal comune*, con una attenzione maniacale/autistica alle eco e all'effetto complessivo della musica nell'ambiente circostante e non solo alle note che emette lo strumento, un *ascolto onnisciente*, incubato nella chiesa di Ohrdruf, fu un *dono della solitudine e del silenzio*.

La famosa improvvisazione di J.S. Bach somma la ricca *immaginazione* melodica al suo estremo *controllo* uditivo: era in grado di immaginare l'effetto di ogni elemento suonato sovrapposto a quelli suonati prima, rimbalzati sulle pareti, e a quelli ancora da suonare, nella sua testa. Questa modalità esecutiva coincide con l'essenza del canone e le due eco delle Hallenkirchen impongono canoni a tre voci.

Spazio-tempo. Analizzando I canoni nascosti nelle diverse Suite di Bach (quelle Francesi e Inglesi o quelle per Violoncello, Violino o Flauto) ci si accorge che il ritardo tra le voci varia generalmente da un quarto di secondo a mezzo secondo circa, questo corrisponde ad una lunghezza di navata tra i quaranta e gli ottanta metri, molto verosimile. I primi pezzi di organo che scrisse Bach, per esempio la Fuga in Do BWV Anh.107, o la Fantasia in Do maggiore BWV 570 celano anch'essi dei canoni. Questo supporta abbastanza bene la mia teoria seguente: suppongo che *l'allenamento dell'udito e le prime esperienze di improvvisazione di Bach ebbero luogo a Ohrdruf, mentre l'elaborazione cosciente e l'affinamento tecnico si fecero nei gli anni seguenti* di studio a Lüneburg e nei primi anni di lavoro. Non ho ancora avuto il piacere di analizzare le composizioni di Dieterich Buxtehude, che Bach era andato a spiare a Lubecca, e che usava intensamente la struttura della fuga, ma non penso di poter trovare canoni multipli nascosti: è certamente un'invenzione di Bach, basata sulla sua esperienza di vita. Anche la tecnica esecutiva basata su canoni immanenti (nascosti) spiega pienamente il successo di J.S. Bach nelle competizioni di improvvisazione: adattava il suono emesso con quello che tornava indietro nello spazio, ottenendo armonie ricche, suoni nitidi e chiari. Questo divenne l'*ingrediente segreto* delle composizioni di J.S. Bach e forse provò ad insegnarlo e trasmetterlo a moglie e figli come si può vedere nelle guide BWV 1072-86 e 1087 che portarono il segreto nella tomba.

Questa ipotesi dell'obiettivo acustico di ottenere un ascolto chiaro e nitido in campi diffusi con eco raggiunto da Bach usando i canoni l'ho validata casualmente ascoltando un concerto di organo in una grande chiesa con una pessima acustica: solo i pezzi di Bach emergevano nitidamente dal confuso rumore di fondo, i pezzi di altri autori annegavano nei rimbombi.

Ad ulteriore supporto devo citare che Bach mostrò un grande **interesse per il fenomeno delle eco**: molte sue composizioni si chiamano Eco (in BVW 821, 831, 1002). Va notato che l'interesse per le eco e il loro utilizzo nei pezzi di musica si riscontra già dal Rinascimento, presso H. Vecchi, A. Banchieri, G. Gabrieli..., o in tempi più prossimi a Bach, presso I. Posch, G. Scronx (Echo in Fa maggiore 1617), S. Scheidt (Echo ad manuale duplex 1624), C. de Tallard (Air in Echo, Suite pour Lute) e più tardi in A. Lotti (Sonata a 4: Echo-Adagio-Presto 1717), A. Vivaldi (RV552, Concerto con violino principale con altro per eco 1740) e in dozzine di compositori più recenti nella storia della musica, ma potete capire che Bach è l'indiscusso sovrano di tutti loro.

A più riprese J.S. Bach cercò di far aggiungere delle **campanelle sull'organo** di Mühlhausen, quand'era incaricato di seguirne la costruzione e accordatura. Questa idea può sembrare sorprendente: l'organo comprende già diverse tastiere e registri, è ricco di timbri e suoni diversi. Questa ida gli veniva dall'organo di Arnstadt che aveva il Cymbelstern (carosello di campanelli), ma a differenza del Cymbelstern, che ruotava automaticamente e muoveva le campanelle con l'aria che usciva dai tubi, in modo casuale e caotico, Bach voleva che le campanelle fossero controllate da una tastiera, suonate da martelletti come le corde di un clavicembalo. A parte il gusto per l'ordine e la precisione, la mia interpretazione come acustico è che gli servisse un suono molto diverso da quello dell'organo, con un attacco molto preciso nel tempo, per regolarsi rispetto alle eco presenti nella chiesa e gestire la sua improvvisazione con canoni nascosti.

Un **assaggio di pignoleria**: l'obiezione scientifica a questa tesi potrebbe essere che le differenti eco generalmente non tornano indietro ad intervalli di tempo regolari (cioè le due eco citate non hanno lo stesso ritardo), specialmente se le dimensioni della sala, o la distanza della sorgente sonora (suonatore) dalle pareti non sono quelle giuste. Posso solo supporre e concludere che nella chiesa di Ohrdruf (andata distrutta da incendi) la posizione dell'organo e le dimensioni erano tali da garantire la situazione suddetta: per esempio se l'organo si trovava all'estremità della navata centrale e se questa era due volte più grande dell'altezza della chiesa, allora le eco avrebbero avuto la distribuzione regolare nel tempo richiesta. Concedetemi un'ultima pignoleria: i pezzi che ho analizzato massicciamente (le Suites) non sono per organo/musica da chiesa, ma da sala, del **periodo di Weimar** (1708-1717) e Köthen, quindi immagino che anche nelle sale del palazzo ducale riscontrasse problemi simili a quelli della chiesa di Ohrdruf. L'opera di Bach per organo deve essere analizzata in modo più esteso riguardo ai canoni nascosti per confermare pienamente la mia tesi sull'origine del "fenomeno Bach" nella chiesa di Ohrdruf. Una genesi nel periodo di Weimar sarebbe più semplice da sostenere, perché nella musica da camera si può scegliere la posizione del suonatore in modo strategico da un punto di vista acustico, mentre per l'organo no.

6   Memoria acustica ed effetto psicoacustico

6.1 La memoria acustica

Secondo dei concetti di base della psicoacustica, la memoria acustica delle persone normali è molto breve, specialmente riferita a rumori insensati: per esempio se si vogliono comparare i rumori di due configurazioni di un veicolo bisogna fare le prove in stretta successione, oppure bisogna registrare e confrontare il suono in cuffia. Per altri suoni, legati alla sopravvivenza umana, grazie all'evoluzione fisiologica, l'udito è molto più sensibile e può cogliere piccole variazioni nel rumore abituale circostante, dal rumore di una zanzara allo scricchiolio di una foglia secca, alla disfunzione di un macchinario. In generale quando una informazione o una emozione sono associate all'ascolto il cervello è più preciso e attento. Parlando di orecchi allenati, dei musicisti non hanno problemi a distinguere degli intervalli di un 24° di ottava (quarto di tono), o a ricordarsi una melodia, o un pezzo di musica complesso in termini di frequenze (armonie) e avvenimenti temporali (ritmi) ed alcuni riescono a ricordarsi le frequenze in modo assoluto, o a valutare se l'ampiezza sonora sia aumentata o diminuita a distanza di tempo. Questo fornisce loro la capacità di regolare la dinamica esecutiva in ampiezza e velocità. Possono anche ricordarsi intere ore di musica. Lo stesso accade agli attori con i testi di poesia, o teatro e a molti religiosi con libri di testi sacri imparati a memoria.

D'altra parte si può osservare che anche persone non allenate si possono ricordare melodie, o poesie corte, o frasi appena sentite e che *l'interpretazione del suono ascoltato richiede tempo*, per esempio per il linguaggio, quando diverse persone parlano contemporaneamente e che è necessario seguire tutti i discorsi. In altri termini si può dire che il suono utile è "conservato vivo" nel cervello per un certo lasso di tempo, come se risuonasse in una camera riverberante, in una specie di spazio di *memoria interpretativa*. Tornando al paese di Bach si può osservare (e

Charlie Chaplin l'ha fatto alla grande, nel "Grande Dittatore"!) che la struttura grammaticale delle frasi in tedesco che ne sospende la determinazione del senso fino al verbo finale, richiede una memoria interpretativa più lunga. Questo tempo di elaborazione sistematico ed inconscio nel nostro cervello esiste tanto per la parola che per la musica: questo significa che *mentre ascoltiamo un suono, il suono precedente è presente nella nostra memoria e coesiste.*

6.2 *La seconda intuizione di Bach*

Penso che Bach abbia osservato e capito questa dinamica mentale al tempo di Ohrdruf (dove Ohr significa orecchio e Ruf significa richiamo, e che quindi era il posto ideale per una vocazione per l'udito di Bach!). Ipotizzo che lui abbia portato ad uno stato cosciente e controllato un fenomeno che per gli altri è inconscio e che l'abbia utilizzato per vincere le sue gare di improvvisazione ed ottenere effetti armonici e sensazioni straordinarie nel cervello degli ascoltatori, dove la musica accompagna e arricchisce sé stessa grazie alla memoria interpretativa.

Siccome la memoria interpretativa acustica non dipende dalla presenza fisica di eco nel luogo di ascolto, l'efficacia dell'approccio di Bach riguarda l'esperienza uditiva comune. Questa seconda parte della mia tesi potrebbe quindi essere considerata come una negazione della prima parte: nessun problema di eco da risolvere, niente acustica delle sale, solo funzionamento psicoacustico del cervello e intuito geniale di Bach.

Preferisco pensare che entrambe le spiegazioni coesistono, perché mi piacciono entrambe e con le idee non sono monogamo. Ho sperimentato personalmente quella fisica (acustica delle sale) e la seconda (quella psicoacustica) è in teoria più difficile da dimostrare (non ho ancora vivisezionato musicologi!), ma potete sperimentarla da voi, concentrandovi su quello che ascoltate e su quello che risuona nella vostra memoria mentre ascoltate i pezzi di Bach.

Ad ogni buon conto, anche considerando solo la spiegazione psichica, l'indicazione di mantenere un tempo di esecuzione stabile quando suonate questi pezzi di Bach resta valida.

6.3 La strategia soggiacente ai canoni nascosti nelle Suites

Quando ho scoperto i primi canoni a tre o sette voci nelle Suites (per Violoncello, Violino, o Flauto), pensavo che si trattasse di una strategia geniale di Bach per ottenere l'effetto di un concerto polifonico con un solo strumento melodico, molto utile ed economico per i viaggi della corte del Principe Leopold di Köthen. Questo era probabilmente un "effetto secondario", non sapevo ancora che Bach aveva messo canoni multipli nascosti nei suoi lavori precedenti di Weimar: le Suite Inglesi e Francesi per clavicembalo! A questo si aggiunge che avrebbe continuato a comporre così anche in seguito, per formazioni più grandi: diversi concerti per orchestra e solisti contengono canoni multipli nascosti. Quindi l'ipotesi dei "kit da viaggio" decadeva completamente ed era necessario trovare una spiegazione: la tesi esposta precedentemente sull'effetto di chiarezza e nitidezza sonora ottenuta in ambienti ostili (acustica delle sale) e l'arricchimento delle sensazioni di ascolto (psicoacustica).

6.4 Perché nascosti per tutto questo tempo?

Le Suite per strumenti soli sono i pezzi di Bach dove si possono scoprire più facilmente i canoni nascosti; mi è quindi capitato come violoncellista, ma anche grazie alla passione per l'analisi dei testi e dei contesti storico-filosofici che mi ha trasmesso mio zio, all'interesse per le Religioni e la psicologia che mi ha lasciato mio padre, alla comprensione scientifica dei fenomeni acustici che mi ha dato un dottorato, alla familiarità ingegneristica con i computer, ad un metodo compositivo contrappuntistico metamusicale [11] e ad una certa insistenza autistica. È sempre l'esito, il risultato che attira a sé tutti gli elementi necessari, in modi imprevedibili, incoerenti e improbabili. Il Principe Leopold da buon Calvinista avrebbe parlato di predestinazione, di universo necessario.

Perché nessuno si è accorto di questi canoni multipli nascosti nelle melodie di Bach per tre secoli? Cercherò di dare qualche possibile spiegazione: le Suite di danze erano una forma che cadde in disuso, le danze di corte, effimere e mondane, cambiarono, quelle proposte da Bach erano inutilizzabili, poi la musica per strumenti soli si spostò dalle corti ai salotti borghesi, imbottiti e senza eco, i pezzi di Bach, simboli di equilibrio e armonia, benché virtuosi, non erano di gusto abbastanza romantico e per i musicisti di strada gli spartiti erano troppo costosi.

Ciò nonostante le Suite di Bach furono studiate da grandi compositori come Mendelssohn, e la musica di Bach influenzò Haydn, Mozart, Beethoven e molti compositori successivi, ma nessuno notò i canoni raffinati né il ritratto-testamento. La fuga sembrava più complessa e sfidante per un compositore e per i musicologi. Questo oblio rivela anche che nessuno dei familiari di Bach svelò mai l'ingrediente segreto della "ditta", malgrado lo stato di povertà di Anna Magdalena: probabilmente l'avevano giurato, o non l'hanno mai saputo. Bisognerebbe studiare i loro pezzi ...

Anche nella nostra epoca tardo romantica i solisti come Casals, Glenn Gould, che hanno passato la loro vita con le Suite, ne hanno sfruttato la bellezza al fine di esprimere il loro talento, senza notare i tesori che nascondevano. D'altro canto è veramente difficile astrarsi dall'attrazione e dal piacere che suscitano suonandole, le melodie cambiano continuamente di stile e di atmosfera e non si può pensare che siano canoni.

6.5 *Ultima revisione delle Suites*

Dopo aver formulato la spiegazione fisica del gioco con le eco, ho rimesso in questione le mie prime analisi sulle Suites per violoncello: i ritardi delle voci nel tempo erano troppo lunghi rispetto alle Suites che ho analizzato in seguito e rispetto alle dimensioni delle sale. Ho così trovato delle soluzioni con ritardi più brevi che non impongono nessun cambiamento nei Preludi della seconda Suite e della prima Suite. Tutte le ipotesi sui "buchi" lasciati negli spartiti e completati da Anna Magdalena, dei paragrafi 2.5 e 2.6, benché seducenti e divertenti, con queste nuove soluzioni non sono più necessarie. L'inizio della seconda Suite diventa quindi:

Tutto questo lavoro sarebbe quindi nato da un ascolto errato del Preludio della seconda Suite, fatto secondo le abitudini di cantare canoni con ritardi di una battuta circa: un errore comunque fecondo, senza il quale i veri canoni non sarebbero tornati alla luce. Ho rianalizzato vari brani e messo le nuove versioni degli spartiti sui siti IMSLP e AIMAmusic.

Bisogna anche notare che i ritardi brevi tra le voci limitano le sovrapposizioni tra diverse tonalità a segmenti di musica più brevi e facilitano la composizione dei canoni multipli evolutivi e modulanti. L'ascolto dei ritardi brevi non ha niente di intuitivo, è difficile e fa emergere l'eccezionalità dell'udito di J.S. Bach.

7 Conclusioni

1. Ho trovato un tesoro nascosto seguendo la mappa viva di uno spartito, dopo secoli di attesa paziente del compositore: dei preziosi canoni multipli evolutivi e modulanti sono incastonati come diamanti e smeraldi, immanenti, invisibili, in molti capolavori di J.S. Bach.

2. Facendo questo, "en passant" ho capito meglio il senso dello strano viaggio della mia vita.

3. Adesso tutti possono ascoltare la complessità di come Bach concepiva il suo lavoro, riscoprire i suoi capolavori estranianti ed esplorare nuove capacità della propria mente.

4. I musicisti possono suonare insieme, o da soli, con qualche ausilio audio, e trovare nuovi modi di interpretare dei classici. Anche clonare musicisti adesso può avere senso!

5. I musicisti forse faranno più attenzione scegliendo la posizione dove suonano o ascoltano la musica di Bach in una sala acusticamente ostile.

6. I musicologi possono continuare le ricerche sulle opere di Bach e scoprire altri mondi inaspettati, oppure sprecare un po' di tempo per invalidare questo lavoro se loro aggrada.

7. E se è stato solo un sogno, ne è stato uno magnifico, degno invero d'essere sognato!

RIFERIMENTI per gli SPARTITI dei CANONI NASCOSTI

[A] Cello Suites https://imslp.org/wiki/File:PMLP4291-6CelloSuitesHiddenCanonsGuide.pdf
[B] Violin Suites best of
https://imslp.org/wiki/Special:ImagefromIndex/790271/vg25
[C] "completed" Flute Suite
https://imslp.org/wiki/Special:ImagefromIndex/788474/vg25
[D] "completed" French Suites
https://imslp.org/wiki/Special:ImagefromIndex/809911/vg25
[E] English Suites
https://imslp.org/wiki/Special:ImagefromIndex/809741/vg25
[F] Goldberg Variations Aria
https://imslp.org/wiki/Special:ImagefromIndex/809278/vg25
[G] Violin Concerto BWV 1041
https://imslp.org/wiki/Special:ImagefromIndex/821336/vg25
[H] 2 Violins Concerto BWV 1043
https://imslp.org/wiki/Special:ImagefromIndex/821337/vg25
[I] Oboe and Violin Concerto BWV 1060R
https://imslp.org/wiki/Special:ImagefromIndex/821335/vg25
[J] 5th Brandenburger BWV 1050 Allegro
https://imslp.org/wiki/Special:ImagefromIndex/822690/vg25

ASCOLTI in RETE

https://www.youtube.com/channel/UCG4BI8Q1vR7SbMxCxDJ_yIA

https://metamusica.altervista.org/

Mini Bibliografia

[1.a] Denis Collins, *From Bull to Bach: In Search of Precedents for the "Complete" Version of the Canon by Augmentation and Contrary Motion in J. S. Bach's "Musical Offering"* Source: Bach, Vol. 38, No. 2 (2007), pp. 39-63 Published by: Riemenschneider Bach Institute.

[1.b] Dennis Collins and W. Andrew Schloss, *An Unusual Effect in the Canon Per Tonos from J. S. Bach's Musical Offering* Source: Music Perception: An Interdisciplinary Journal, Vol. 19, No. 2 (Winter 2001), pp. 141-153 Published by: University of California Press

[1.c] Denis Collins, *Bach and Approaches to Canonic Composition in Early Eighteenth-Century Theoretical and Chamber Music Sources*. Source: Bach, Vol. 30, No. 2 (1999), pp. 27-48 Published by: Riemenschneider Bach Institute

[2] Marcel Bitsch , *J.S. Bach, canons BWV 1087: analyse et commentaires* 1977, Durand, T. Presse

[3] Christoph Wolff, "Bach's Handexemplar of the Goldberg Variations: A New Source", Journal of the American Musicological Society XXIV/2 (Summer 1976), pp. 224-241.

[4] Denis Collins *Historical precedents for Bach's "evolutio" canon BWV1087/10* Source: Bach, vol. 24, No. 1 (Spring-Summer, 1993), pp. 5-14 Published by: Riemenschneider Bach Institute

[5] Alexander Maykapar, September 2, 2015 THE 13th CANON: Portrait of J.S. Bach In https://www.projectawe.org/blog?category=AWE https://www.projectawe.org/blog?category=maria+danova

[6a] Athanase Papadopoulos, *Mathématiques et musique chez J.S. Bach*, 2000, L'ouvert 100, papadopoulos@math.u-strasbg.fr

[6b] Martin Jarvis, *Written by Mrs Bach*, 2011, HarperCollins Publishers Australia. http://www.harpercollins.com.au/9780733328725/

[7] Tony Phillips, *Math and the Musical Offering*, https://www.ams.org/publicoutreach/feature-column/fcarc-canons

[8] J.S. Bach Crab Canon on a Moebius band https://www.openculture.com/2009/09/how_a_bach_canon_works.html

[9a] Denis Collins, *Bach's Occasional Canon BWV 1073 and "Stacked" Canonic Procedure in the Eighteenth Century* Source: Bach, Vol. 33, No. 2 (2002), pp. 15-34 Published by: Riemenschneider Bach Institute

[9b] Albert Clement, *Johann Sebastian Bach and the praise of God, some thoughts on the canon triplex (BWV 1076),* In: Music and theology: essays in honor of Robin A. Leaver/ed. by Daniel Zager-Lanham, Md.[u.a.], 2007.- S. 147-168

[10] Dr. Timothy A. Smith, Northern Arizona University *Canons and Fugues of J.S. Bach*, Tutorial 2020-2021

[11] https://metamusica.altervista.org/spiegazioni/generalinfo.html

[12] Bob van Asperen, contrib. F. Huneau, M. Quagliozzi, *François Dieupart's Biography Revised and the Genesis and Dating of his Six Suittes de Clavessin, with Remarks on their Influence on J.S. Bach.* Amsterdam, 2021

[13] John Eliot Gardiner, *Bach: Music in the Castle of Heaven,* 2013

Informazioni sull'autore

Giovanni Pietro Orefice (Milano 1967-Gap-Grenoble-Lyon-Berlin-Paris-Torino-Milano/Desenzano/Modena), Dottorato in Acustica, Violoncellista, Compositore di Metamusica (cf [11]).

Les secrets des canons cachés dans les chefs-d'œuvre de J.S. Bach

Büchlein für Johann Sebastian

Introduction

En écoutant la musique du grand compositeur J.S. Bach, tout mélomane peut ressentir une profonde résonance de ses mélodies dans son âme. De plus, si, dans une église réverbérante, on compare ses chefs-d'œuvre pour orgue à ceux d'autres compositeurs, les siens se distinguent par une clarté impressionnante. Dans ce petit livre, je vais essayer d'approfondir et d'expliquer ces deux expériences, en m'appuyant sur le travail de dévoilement des canons cachés dans de nombreuses pièces célèbres de J.S. Bach.

Pour que ce texte reste compréhensible, j'ai évité les technicismes des articles spécialisés en musicologie. L'objectif est d'inspirer les musiciens et les musicologues, de leur fournir de nombreuses idées pour des recherches plus orthodoxes et d'être un guide pour tous les fans de la musique de Bach, qui découvriront la beauté des canons multiples dans les pièces indiquées et trouveront une explication des sensations indescriptibles qu'ils ressentent à l'écoute de ses œuvres.

Contre toute attente, trois siècles après sa composition, l'œuvre de J.S. Bach recèle encore de nombreuses surprises et trésors cachés. La première partie de ce petit livre présente la recherche musicologique que j'ai menée sur ce monstre sacré de l'histoire de la musique, pour révéler la structure immanente de canon multiple cachée dans son œuvre, structure jusque-là inconnue. J'ai commencé cette découverte à partir des Suites pour violoncelle seul, en continuant avec les Sonates et Partitas pour violon seul, avec la Suite incomplète pour Flûte, avec les Suites françaises et anglaises pour clavecin, en ajoutant quelques

Préludes pour la compléter et j'ai terminé en explorant quelques concertos pour orchestre et instruments solistes. Ce travail a aussi révélé des effets rythmiques inattendus et des parties manquantes dans certaines pièces, je propose des pistes pour les compléter et des solutions à d'anciens conflits et problèmes d'attribution. Je vais essayer d'expliquer la difficulté de composer des canons multiples et de fournir quelques comparaisons avec des pièces d'autres auteurs célèbres de l'époque pour apporter un nouvel éclairage sur Bach, dont le talent est encore sous-estimé, comme nous allons le découvrir.

Dans la seconde partie de ce petit livre je présenterai une thèse innovante, issue des connaissances de la physique acoustique et psychoacoustique acquises par mes études et mon métier, avec l'apport de mon expérience et de ma réflexion de musicien interprète. Cette approche particulière fournit une explication des motivations pratiques et tactiques de J.S. Bach de dissimuler de façon omniprésente dans ses lignes mélodiques les canons multiples présentés dans la première partie. Cette théorie nous permet de clarifier comment Bach, en tant qu'improvisateur et compositeur, a résolu certains problèmes typiques des interprètes, obtenant un avantage concurrentiel dans ses célèbres et glorieux tournois d'improvisation. La thèse affirme également que Bach a instinctivement compris certains effets psychoacoustiques et a décidé d'adopter cet ingrédient secret pour composer des chefs-d'œuvre et obtenir un succès mondial éternel.

Si vous n'êtes pas intéressés par les détails techniques des structures canoniques et les étapes du processus de découverte des canons cachés, mais voulez comprendre pourquoi J.S. Bach les a cachés, passez directement à la deuxième partie de ce petit livre, mais lire quelques pages de plus ne vous tuera pas (tout comme ces canons !)

1ère Partie CANONS QUI NE TUENT PAS

1   Canons explicites ou cachés, immanents

Pour les détails de la découverte des canons cachés, passez au chapitre 2. Le but de ce chapitre est de faire la distinction entre les canons explicites et visibles dans les compositions de Bach et les canons cachés qui seront traités dans le 2ème chapitre.

Compréhension habituelle des canons de J.S. Bach

Les canons les plus célèbres et les plus développés de Bach sont les dix écrits explicitement dans l'Offrande musicale BWV 1079 pour le roi de Prusse, cf [1], dont Anton Webern a développé le Ricercare pour 6 voix en 1935. Bach a également écrit la variation en canon sur "Von Himmel hoch" (pour orgue) BWV 769 comme lettre d'introduction à la Société Mizler de Leipzig, dont il devint membre en 1747. Ces deux ouvrages montrent à quel point la forme du canon était importante pour lui et combien il appréciait sa capacité à jongler avec elle, à tel point qu'il la considérait comme sa carte de visite et même comme un cadeau digne d'un monarque. D'autre part, nous trouvons aussi un canon dans le petit livre (Büchlein) pour Anna Magdalena (Canon, BWV Anh.120), un recueil de perles musicales, un canon devient ainsi un cadeau et gage suprême d'amour.

A côté des pièces musicales précédentes, ses courts canons BWV 1072-86 sont généralement considérés et classés comme matériel pédagogique pour ses enfants et élèves, ou comme exercices/pièces de circonstance (BWV 1073), ou, à l'inverse, sanctifiés (canon triplex BWV 1076) [9].

Je reporte en exemple le premier canon dans la Fig.1.

Figure 1: BWV 1072 Kanon zu acht Stimmen. On peut observer ici que la ligne mélodique oscille, comme une onde sinusoïdale et que quatre voix restent à l'intérieur des mesures tandis que quatre autres voix (intermédiaires) ont des notes à cheval et créent une certaine complexité rythmique en contre-temps. Les mêmes éléments peuvent être répétés à l'infini (canon circulaire). Une neuvième voix serait identique à la première.

Toujours dans l'Art de la fugue BWV 1080, Bach a clairement déployé des canons à 4 voix et des structures complexes (canon à la douzième en contrepoint à la quinte, deux canons "per augmentationem in contra motu") et ils ne sont pas considérés comme de simples exercices, mais comme des morceaux de musique à tout point de vue.

La découverte des 14 canons BWV 1087, trouvés seulement en 1974 à la fin de la copie personnelle de Bach des Variations Goldberg BWV988, sur une seule page, a révélé au monde à quel point la structure du canon pouvait être raffinée et complexe dans son esprit, avec des variantes à symétrie horizontale et verticale (sur la partition) et l'exploration des dilatations et des contractions du temps, ajoutées au décalage dans le temps typique des canons. Cette feuille unique (cf. Fig.2) est un véritable Guide des canons, largement expliqué, commenté et illustré, cf. [2], [3], [4], [5].

De plus, le canon 13 correspond à celui représenté dans le portrait par J.S. Bach réalisé par Elias Gottlob Haussmann (1746), cette précieuse page contenait donc ce qu'il considérait comme l'héritage le plus important de sa vie : un testament musical !

Figure 2: BWV 1087 Holograph manuscript, n.d.(ca.1741-46)
https://imslp.org/wiki/File:PMLP326356-N55005962_(BWV_1087).pdf

Comme "conséquence", ou effet secondaire de cette découverte, des "études" (telles que [6a], [7], [8]) sont apparues sur les transformées mathématiques qui décrivent les processus d'écriture des canons : mais ces travaux peuvent au mieux servir à développer de nouveaux outils dans les logiciels d'aide à la composition et n'apportent aucune connaissance musicale/musicologique intéressante.

En 1867, Helfer, Friedrich August avec son Canon für 2 Clav. tu. Pedal BACH über Bach, In: Album für die Orgel zu J. G.Töpfer's goldner Amts-Jubelfeier am 4. Juni 1867. - Weimar: T. F. A. Kühn, 1867, p. 54-55, a exploré un canon caché dans une pièce d'orgue.

Malgré toutes ces publications, la capacité de J.S. Bach à composer des canons multiples dans ses chefs-d'œuvre n'a été que partiellement goûtée que dans le 10ème morceau de l'Offrande musicale BWV 1079 (Canon a 4 quaerendo invenietis) et n'a jamais été découverte et appréciée de son vivant: le roi guerrier de Prusse n'a pas été très impressionné au cours de sa visite, on lui avait peut-être promis un expert de canons et il avait pensé à ses chers canons de guerre ! Plus sérieusement les enseignements théoriques que J.S. Bach a laissés dans les pièces ci-dessus, ses guides et ses petits livres pour ses enfants et sa femme bien-aimés ne semblent pas avoir eu une application complète dans ses pièces majeures et son estime des canons en tant que forme la plus élevée de création n'a jamais été pleinement comprise...

Jusqu'ici je n'ai parlé que des canons explicites, visibles dans les différentes œuvres, plus ou moins faciles à entendre et à reconnaître (moins maintenant, grâce aux vidéos pédagogiques [10]) et bien connus des musicologues et de nombreux musiciens. Au contraire, le thème de ce livre sont les canons immanents, insoupçonnés, inconnus et cachés dans de nombreuses œuvres, qui sont restés secrets et que je ramène à la lumière de notre intellect après trois siècles d'inattention difficile à expliquer et tout à fait impardonnable.

2 Le dévoilement des canons cachés de Bach : une aventure passionnée

2.1 Quelques mots sur les Suites de J.S. Bach

La Suite de danses est une forme musicale qui reflète une double influence française sur J.S. Bach. La plus évidente est la fascination qu'il éprouvait (lui et plus généralement toutes les petites cours germanophones) pour la grande Cour du Roi Soleil Louis XIV, avec ses danses qui donnaient une représentation physique de la domination absolue du Roi sur les nobles et les dames de cour. Une autre influence plus subtile est celle philosophique, qui à partir de Descartes (et en passant par un Spinoza, plus complexe) arriva à Leibniz, qui dominait certainement la pensée et les croyances dans l'aire germanique à l'époque de Bach : la nécessité d'une harmonie universelle, le sens d'un univers structuré, plein d'ordre et de beauté, reflétant la perfection de son créateur divin. Dans les territoires de Bach, l'ordre était apprécié et guidé par l'Église austère de Luther et de Calvin (particulièrement austère après la terrible période de l'extermination des anabaptistes), opposée au monde très différent, incohérent et laxiste de l'Église catholique italienne, qui pourtant avait un côté plein d'imagination et de liberté, d'ornements virtuoses et d'effets spéciaux, de grands concerts baroques qui ont certainement fasciné et inspiré Bach dans ses compositions et ses improvisations.

La suite de danse baroque débute par une Ouverture, suivie d'une alternance de danses d'intensité et de vitesse différentes, pour doser l'effort physique et éviter la sueur plébéienne. On retrouve typiquement l'Allemande, la Courante, la Sarabande et la Gigue.

Après le 17ème siècle d'autres danses ont été intégrées et insérées, comme les Menuets, les Bourrées, les Gavottes, les Passepieds, les Rigaudons... Quant aux Suites pour Violoncelle, un précurseur et référence célèbre fut Marin Marais (1656-1728) avec ses Pièces de viole, qui ont certainement influencé l'œuvre de Bach : le premier livre de ces Pièces (1686) était en fait une Suite très complète (Prélude - Fantaisie - Allemande - Double - Courante - Double - Sarabande - Gigue - Double) et explique l'utilisation des noms « Double » et « Phantasie » dans ses compositions. La *Suitte d'un Goût Étranger* de Marin Marais ne comptait pas moins de 33 danses !

Bach a toujours ajouté quelques "danses galantes" dans les Suites pour violoncelle, ou doublé une autre pièce comme la Courante, ou inséré une paire de pièces jumelles appelées "Doubles", ou une danse exotique comme la Sicilienne, ou même en omettant le nom (lui, ou sa femme, ou un copiste) de certains morceaux des Partitas et Sonates pour Violon en ne laissant que l'indication de vitesse/caractère (Presto, Adagio, Largo, Allegro etc.…).

J.S. Bach, comme Marin Marais, proposa ses Suites pour instrument soliste comme une brillante forme de divertissement pour une petite cour, dans le style idéal de la somptueuse Versailles, mais avec la modique dépense d'un seul musicien pour toute une séance de danses, comme dans les Cours de la Renaissance, avec leurs ménestrels errants.

Incontournables chez Bach, sont les Préludes, souvent enrichis de la complexité d'une Fugue, pour leur intérêt musical avec leur double rôle de préparation aux danses et d'accompagnement musical d'un moment de discussions, tel le "piano bar" moderne. Outre l'aspect formel de ces danses, l'œuvre précieuse de Bach exprime clairement sa structure robuste et présente des mélodies qui pénètrent l'âme de l'auditeur et traduisent la beauté de l'univers en son. Il y a diverses discussions parmi les musicologues sur le style des danses, qu'elles soient plutôt italiennes ou françaises, mais l'important est l'intention globale et idéale des Suites : même les « Suites anglaises » ont été composées et offertes avec l'intention et l'espoir d'être appréciées à la Cour d'Angleterre, mais toujours pour recréer l'atmosphère et la splendeur de la Cour de France.

On peut également faire une distinction entre les Suites pour clavecin, instrument polyphonique, autonome et harmoniquement complet, composées avant la période de Köthen (et inspirées peut-être par celles de François Dieupart, cf [12]), et celles pour Violoncelle/Violon/Flûte, qui représentaient un défi compositionnel (lancé par Marin Marais), car elles devaient animer une séance de danses à l'aide d'un seul instrument mélodique, avec le problème de marquer le rythme, ce qui était plus courant dans la musique de rue, dans les tavernes ou sur les bateaux, que dans les cours princières où elles risquaient d'être insuffisantes. On peut émettre l'hypothèse que ces Suites sont nées comme un « kit de voyage » pour le prince itinérant Léopold de Köthen, afin de minimiser le nombre et le coût des musiciens impliqués dans les voyages.

Dernier constat : le caractère méditatif et vagabond de nombre des pièces pour violon et violoncelle que nous avons à l'esprit aujourd'hui est un héritage déformant des interprétations romantiques tardives des siècles passés, qui considéraient ces Suites comme de pures musiques de salon, sans rapport avec les danses, ou comme de simples exercices techniques (!). Au cours des dernières décennies, divers interprètes ont montré combien les danses des Suites peuvent être jouées pleinement comme des danses, avec leur caractère rythmique original. Les Suites pour clavecin ont moins souffert de cette déformation romantique.

2.2 Dévoilement des secrets de la 2ème Suite "a Violoncello Solo senza basso"

2.2.1 Le Prélude de la deuxième Suite

En 1984, alors que j'étais lycéen, il m'est arrivé de jouer les Suites pour violoncelle dans une pièce aux murs de bois (une petite chapelle dans les Alpes françaises, assez réverbérante et résonnante) et j'ai été frappé par un effet sonore étrange : en jouant, j'avais l'impression de m'auto-accompagner. Je me suis promis d'approfondir la question.

À l'été 1991, en jouant le Prélude de la 2e Suite, en écoutant attentivement et en chantant le début de cette pièce mélodique, je me suis rendu compte que cela fonctionnait parfaitement en canon. Après une brève analyse écrite, j'ai réalisé que tout le Prélude fonctionnait comme un canon. J'ai de suite (mal) développé les accords finaux pour que la mélodie respecte la structure en canon et j'ai imprimé le morceau en duo, à jouer pour deux violoncelles, ou avec violon (dans l'octave) et violoncelle. Quelques années

Figure 3: 2ème Suite, canon à deux voix

plus tard, en le testant avec un ami, il a constaté que certaines pièces ne fonctionnaient pas correctement, alors je me suis promis de les réparer au plus vite. En 2019 (!) J'ai finalement recopié la pièce sur un ordinateur avec un nouveau logiciel de base et j'ai vu qu'il y avait en effet plusieurs mesures problématiques. Il m'a fallu du temps pour proposer une solution en canon, car cela nécessitait une transformation complète de la mélodie. Au passage, je commençais à me demander pourquoi Bach n'avait pas composé ces mesures en canon comme le reste du morceau. Incapable de trouver une réponse, j'ai repris l'analyse de la pièce et j'ai vu visuellement qu'il y avait de la place pour une troisième voix dans le canon : j'ai tout de suite essayé et ça a marché ! J'expliquerai plus tard que, comme je venais de mettre les pieds dans un monde beaucoup plus complexe, maintenant il fallait beaucoup plus de temps et d'efforts pour trouver une solution aux mesures problématiques et le développement des accords finaux devait également être peaufiné. De plus, quelle qu'ait été la solution que je trouvais (ce n'est pas un problème à solution unique) elle était musicalement insatisfaisante par rapport au reste de l'original de Bach. Enfin, pour le canon à trois voix, il a fallu aussi corriger quelques notes sporadiques dans le reste du morceau, en dévastant la linéarité mélodique. Encore plus récemment en 2023 j'ai essayé de trouver de meilleures solutions (notamment pour le développement des accords finaux), mais la série de mesures problématiques résiste encore : elles restent un bon exercice si vous voulez vous essayer !

Mon explication de la raison pour laquelle cette section de la pièce originale (identique dans les versions d'Anna Magdalena et de Kellner) ne fonctionnait pas dans le canon était que J.S. Bach avait composé la Suite juste après la mort subite de sa femme et qu'il avait laissé un "trou" en correspondance avec les sections et à la fin du morceau, avec quelques indications d'accords, à "compléter plus tard". Il n'a probablement jamais trouvé le courage de terminer cette pièce car il l'a douloureusement associée au deuil et la pièce a été complétée et corrigée par la phantasie et l'élégance d'Anna Magdalena Wilcke. Une autre version possible est que personne ne comprenait pourquoi il lui fallait tant de temps pour terminer une simple pièce pour violoncelle seul et qu'il devait la boucler rapidement, parmi d'autres compositions, pour la vendre, mais je ne pense pas, car les Suites ont été publiées seulement plusieurs années plus tard. Peut-être devait-il les donner à son élève Kellner, ou à un autre violoncelliste lors d'un bal de cour, en tout cas l'intention initiale probable d'être un cadeau pour le prince Léopold, qui jouait de la viole de gambe, avait été mise de côté, car le prince n'était certainement pas un grand musicien et les Suites n'étaient pas très faciles à jouer, il n'y avait donc pas d'urgence à compléter le "paquet cadeau".

2.2.2   Les accords finaux non développés

Suite à cette découverte, la vieille diatribe entre violoncellistes sur l'opportunité de développer ou non les accords finaux du Prélude de la 2ème Suite est résolue : avec le court intervalle de temps entre les différentes voix, on pourrait même accepter une version raccourcie des accords, comme dans la figure 5, pour éviter qu'ils ne se chevauchent, mais je suis convaincu qu'ils devraient être développés pour compléter le triple canon de manière mélodique et discursive, comme dans l'exemple de la figure 6.

Figure 4: accords de la partition d'origine

Figure 5: accords courts acceptables comme triple canon

Figure 6: exemple de développement des accords en canon à trois voix

2.2.3   Dévoilement du restant de la 2ème Suite

A ce stade je pensais que cette découverte d'un canon à trois voix, caché dans un morceau aussi beau et long que le Prélude, était un remarquable exemplaire unique dans l'histoire de la musique, mais, juste pour le plaisir, j'ai essayé d'étendre l'analyse au deuxième morceau de la Suite, l'Allemande : incroyablement elle aussi était un double canon. Il n'y avait pas de choix, il fallait voir toutes les danses, une par une : la Courante, la Sarabande, la paire de Menuets et la Gigue ont révélé leurs trésors. J'ai dû recopier la partition note par note, profitant du peu de temps des week-ends fin 2021. Heureusement dans les danses il n'y avait pas les problèmes que j'avais rencontrés dans le Prélude, seulement quelques fausses notes à "corriger", mais à chaque triple canon découvert correspondait une grande joie et le plaisir d'entendre quelque chose de nouveau, car, de façon incroyable, même quand on connaît le morceau par cœur et qu'on l'assemble, on ne peut pas imaginer à l'avance comment sonne le contre-canon, et ce pour toute une suite de danses : j'avais été assis sur le coffre au trésor pendant des dizaines d'années sans m'en rendre compte !

Enfin, j'ai partagé les partitions sur quelques sites Web (musique IMSLP et AIMA) et présenté la découverte dans un webinaire.

2.3 Les secrets des autres Suites pour violoncelle

Au cours des premiers mois de 2022, j'ai étendu mes recherches aux autres Suites pour violoncelle, découvrant la même structure cachée du canon à trois voix, jusque dans le Prélude et Fugue insoupçonnable de la cinquième Suite qui a la double structure de contre-canon et de fugue: un chef-d'œuvre absolu ! Le dernier morceau de la dernière Suite, une Gigue, fonctionne même comme un canon à 10 voix ! Je l'ai adapté et simplifié un peu pour un ensemble d'instruments à vent (pour mieux distinguer le timbre de chaque voix).

Il est intéressant de noter que certains passages, ou notes seules, ne satisfont pas au canon à trois voix, par exemple dans le Prélude de la première Suite : peut-être Bach a-t-il laissé un "trou" à combler plus tard, ou un accident a détruit la partition (eau versée sur l'encre, souris qui rongea le papier ?) et quelqu'un (Anna Magdalena ?) a trouvé une mélodie raisonnable pour recoller le tout.

La manière de faire fonctionner le canon est très variée et cela a fait de cette recherche un voyage plein de surprises, avec la récompense d'écouter les effets cachés. J'ai aussi observé que dans chaque Suite il y avait une pièce unique qui fonctionnait même comme un canon à 7 voix (si on tolère des 4èmes et 5èmes parallèles), sans perdre immédiatement la clarté de la structure, une pièce différente pour chacune des six Suites, pièce qui, prise et placée avec les autres exceptions, forme une « septième Suite pour 7 violoncelles ».

Un chercheur [6b] a proposé d'attribuer toutes les Suites pour violoncelle à l'épouse de Bach, mais après cette recherche (voir surtout les paragraphes suivants) je peux affirmer que l'écoute interne des canons à trois (ou plus) voix est une signature de J.S. Bach que personne ne peut imiter. J'expliquerai pourquoi dans la deuxième partie de ce livre.

Dans les annexes j'ai mis l'adresse du guide des canons des suites pour violoncelle (avec le début de chaque morceau et l'intervalle entre les voix) et j'ai mis en ligne un peu d'audio pour donner un avant-goût des canons.

2.4 Découverte des Suites pour autres instruments

Après avoir analysé les 6x7 = 42 morceaux des Suites pour violoncelle, il était maintenant clair pour moi que J.S. Bach était un « canoniste en série »: il avait une façon naturelle et spontanée d'écouter et de composer des mélodies qui cachaient des canons multiples, comme une maladie professionnelle (il en faudrait beaucoup comme celle-là!) pour une raison mystérieuse qu'il fallait que je comprenne.

Pour vérifier cette hypothèse, je devais explorer plus de pièces. Ayant en tête la thèse des "kits de voyage" pour le Prince Léopold, le premier trimestre 2022 j'ai étendu l'analyse aux autres œuvres composées par Bach dans sa cour, des œuvres pour instruments solistes mélodiques : les Suites pour violon et celle pour flûte.

Gardez à l'esprit que lorsque je dis "analyser un morceau", je veux vraiment dire copier patiemment la partition note par note dans l'ordinateur d'une manière similaire à ce que Bach lui-même faisait sur papier lorsqu'il était enfant découvrant les chefs-d'œuvre de ses contemporains, mais sans son stress de ne pouvoir se tromper, de ne pas faire de taches d'encre, de ne pas se casser des plumes et de ne pas gaspiller de papier et d'en être puni ! La deuxième étape est plus facile que ce travail de moine copiste : un simple copier-coller de la première voix sur d'autres portées, à la recherche du bon décalage pour obtenir au moins 80% de recouvrement agréable et formellement sensé. Il y a des façons plus pratiques d'effectuer ce travail (malheureusement je n'y ai pensé que plus tard !) à notre époque moderne : il suffit de trouver un fichier déjà transcrit sur des sites comme musescore, ou de trouver un fichier au format midi et de l'importer dans des traitements de texte musicaux, etc. un travail de disque jokey. C'est beaucoup plus rapide mais on apprend beaucoup moins et surtout à partir des fichiers audios, la retranscription peut être très fausse rythmiquement par rapport à l'original et la partition est complètement altérée. De plus on rate le plaisir de lire les partitions originales manuscrites de Bach et sa famille/compagnie, avec les marques de commentaire, les lignes élégantes suggérant déjà l'interprétation : musique pour les yeux, et on rate tout le plaisir de trouver des erreurs ou des divergences entre les différentes versions, bref, il manque tout le goût de l'Histoire !

À la hâte (dans les Suites pour Violon il y a beaucoup de notes à copier par rapport à celles pour Violoncelle) et courant un certain risque, partant de mon hypothèse numérologique, que j'expliquerai dans un paragraphe spécifique, je me suis concentré directement sur la recherche des " pièces spéciales" des six Sonates et Partitas (BWV 1001-1006) qui fonctionnaient comme des canons à 7 voix, en espérant qu'il y en ait une spéciale pour chaque Suite, comme dans celles pour violoncelle. J'ai commencé par mes morceaux préférés et j'ai vu qu'ils fonctionnaient bien, alors je me suis arrêté là, me suis limité à sept morceaux, que j'ai de nouveau appelés la "Septième Suite Cachée pour Violon Solo". Pour les amis musicologues qui veulent continuer le travail, les autres pièces pour violon sont à votre disposition pour dévoiler leurs contre-canons et les écouter après trois cents ans : je vous assure que ça vaut le coup et que c'est du temps bien investi !

Cela fait, il ne restait que la Partita BWV 1013 pour flûte traversière : l'Allemande, la Courante, la Sarabande, la Bourrée Anglaise révélaient leurs canons cachés à quatre voix. Pour "compléter" cette malheureuse Suite qui semble inachevée, j'ai jeté un œil à d'autres pièces célèbres de Bach pour flûte seule ou accompagnée : il manquait un Prélude, identifié avec la BWV 846 et j'ai ajouté la Badinerie BWV 1067 en pièce finale, révélant leurs canons cachés. Bach avait probablement réutilisé le matériel de flûte solo de la Suite complète pour créer des œuvres plus élaborées et plus réussies. Je dois avouer que le résultat sonore et musical de la Suite pour flûte à plusieurs canons est beaucoup moins satisfaisant et convaincant que celui des Suites pour violon ou violoncelle. Cela peut expliquer pourquoi Bach s'est senti libre de démembrer la Suite et de ne laisser que les restes dans la BWV 1013. Pour enrichir davantage la Suite pour flûte, j'ai récemment analysé la Gigue de la Suite pour luth BWV 997, qui fonctionne comme un canon à 5 voix, et le célèbre Siciliano de la Sonate BWV 1031 qui fonctionne comme un canon à 7 voix.

J'avais alors terminé les Suites pour instruments mélodiques, à voix unique qui pouvaient nécessiter un accompagnement immanent. Mais en écoutant les Suites pour clavier, les Suites Françaises (BWV 812-817) et les Suites Anglaises (BWV 806-811) il m'est apparu que la densité des notes n'était pas très élevée, compte tenu des dix doigts disponibles : bien que parfaites elles étaient assez espacées. Ainsi, pendant les vacances d'été de 2022, j'ai analysé tous les débuts de toutes les pièces des Suites, trouvant la structure cachée d'un canon à trois voix : toutes ces Suites peuvent être jouées par trois clavecins ou pianos. Là aussi j'ai "complété" les Suites françaises avec les Préludes manquants, tirés de ceux "de réserve" préparés par

Bach, en les combinant par tonalité (BWV 935, BWV 934, BWV 925, BWV 876, BWV 816, BWV 937).

L'analyse de ces suites pour clavecin m'en disait long car elles n'avaient pas été écrites à l'époque de Köthen pour le Prince Léopold, mais plus tôt. Par conséquent, mon hypothèse des "Suites de Voyage pour Leopold" n'était pas forcément la bonne ! En tout cas, force est de constater que les partitions pour un seul musicien capables d'animer une soirée dansante restaient commercialement une excellente idée, et que celles pour le clavecin pouvaient être utilisées par Bach lui-même pour d'éventuels voyages. Je pense que les premières Suites composées étaient les Françaises, pour les raisons expliquées dans le paragraphe sur les influences, sans les Préludes, avec l'idée d'en ajouter un différent à chaque représentation, ou de l'improviser, avant de jouer les danses, c'est pourquoi nous trouvons de nombreux Préludes séparés et libres, dans de nombreuses nuances et atmosphères, pour toute occasion.

2.5   *Conséquences sur la façon de jouer les Suites*

À vrai dire, après ces découvertes je pense qu'un musicien peut sans doute continuer à jouer tout seul les Suites dans les salles de concert habituelles, car Bach n'a pas explicité ses canons multiples. Mais maintenant, on peut aussi les jouer en groupe, ou tout seul, à l'aide d'un système audio qui ajoute des échos artificiels, soit en se plaçant dans des environnements riches en échos et en adaptant le temps d'exécution à la salle (comme cela m'est arrivé en 1986) pour faire découvrir à un plus large public les merveilles des canons multiples.

Quant à l'interprétation des suites, les musiciens peuvent continuer à proposer leurs versions romantiques et maniéristes extrêmes, mais ils doivent savoir qu'il est désormais certain que Bach ne les a pas écoutées ainsi. La présence de deux voix supplémentaires est totalement incompatible avec des changements brusques de tempo et avec une respiration excessive entre deux phrases, abusée par des soupirs romantiques. Soyez en sûrs qu'éviter les pauses et adopter un tempo d'exécution stable, ou avec de faibles variations progressives (accélérations et décélérations) est plus conforme à l'intention initiale et à la présence des canons immanents.

Enfin, je dois souligner que jouer les Suites en canon, avec plusieurs instruments, est un excellent exercice musical, car il demande un contrôle précis de la vitesse, auquel on n'est pas habitué lorsqu'on les joue seuls, et une parfaite maîtrise du volume des différentes voix, car les mélodies deviennent aussi des accompagnements : ma suggestion est de toujours jouer la première voix plus fort et d'affaiblir progressivement les autres, A vrai dire, après ces découvertes je pense qu'un musicien peut sans doute continuer à jouer tout seul les Suites dans les salles de concert habituelles, car Bach n'a pas explicité ses canons multiples. Mais maintenant, on peut aussi les jouer en groupe, ou tout seul, à l'aide d'un système audio qui ajoute des échos artificiels, soit en se plaçant dans des environnements riches en échos et en adaptant le temps d'exécution à la salle (comme cela m'est arrivé en 1986) pour faire découvrir à un plus large public les merveilles des canons multiples.

Quant à l'interprétation des suites, les musiciens peuvent continuer à proposer leurs versions romantiques et maniéristes extrêmes, mais ils doivent savoir qu'il est désormais certain que Bach ne les a pas écoutées ainsi. La présence de deux voix supplémentaires est totalement incompatible avec des changements brusques de tempo et avec une respiration excessive entre deux phrases, abusée par des soupirs romantiques. Soyez en surs qu'éviter les pauses et adopter un tempo d'exécution stable, ou avec de faibles variations progressives (accélérations et décélérations) est plus conforme à l'intention initiale et à la présence des canons immanents.

Enfin, je dois souligner que jouer les Suites en canon, avec plusieurs instruments, est un excellent exercice musical, car il demande un contrôle précis de la vitesse, auquel on n'est pas habitué lorsqu'on les joue seuls, et une parfaite maîtrise du volume des différentes voix, car les mélodies deviennent aussi des accompagnements : ma suggestion est de toujours jouer la première voix plus fort et d'affaiblir progressivement les autres, comme c'est le cas avec les échos naturels.

2.6 *Un excursus excentrique sur la numérologie*

Je dois maintenant dédier quelques mots à la numérologie dans les Suites de Bach. C'est un sujet frivole mais qui mérite d'être approfondi. A l'époque de J.S. Bach la numérologie était un savoir important et omniprésent, que chacun assimilait, plus ou moins volontairement, pour construire ses propres habitudes mentales et ses croyances, comme les superstitions, basées sur des expériences personnelles, ou sur des règles et conventions collectives.

Si vous jetez un œil à la liste complète des Suites composées par J.S. Bach (par exemple sur https://en.wikipedia.org/wiki/Suite_(Bach), ou dans les archives officielles de Leipzig), on constate immédiatement qu'elle comporte quelques **ensembles** complets de six Suites : *un* groupe pour violoncelle (BWV 1007-1012), *un* pour violon (BWV 1001-1006), *quatre* pour clavecin (BWV 806-811, BWV 812-817, BWV 825-830, BWV 818-824). Donc **six**. Dans chaque Suite, il y a généralement *six* danses. Vous voyez donc clairement que s'il y avait six ensembles on obtiendrait le "nombre satanique" 666, ce qui est absolument inacceptable pour un champion de la musique sacrée, considérée comme une expression religieuse suprême cf [9b] ; heureusement il y a encore d'autres Suites : les Suites et Ouvertures pour Clavecin (BWV 831, BWV 832-845), ou Luth (BWV 995-998), ou Orchestre (BWV1066-1069-1070), sans oublier les mouvements « de secours » (principalement des Préludes). Comme démenti de poids, j'ajoute que le regroupement en ensembles a été fait après la mort de Bach, il n'y a donc aucune raison de supposer une intention satanique de la part de Bach et vous pouvez aussitôt oublier ce paragraphe.

Mais sur ce thème numérologique il faut rappeler que J.S. Bach était le 7ème de 7 enfants d'une merveilleuse famille qui a construit un paradis musical autour de lui pendant sept ans avant de s'effondrer. De plus, sa formation musicale a eu lieu à l'église Saint-Michel d'Ohrdruf et à l'école Saint-Michel de Lunebourg. Or Saint Michel est l'ange chargé de sonner la première des *sept* trompettes de l'Apocalypse. Il s'ensuit que Bach devait avoir une relation positive avec le chiffre sept, sans compter que dans la culture occidentale le chiffre sept est généralement considéré comme un chiffre porte-bonheur, associé au septième jour, celui du repos, et qui représente ainsi *l'achèvement du cycle de la création* (dans la Bible) et la semaine sainte de la Passion chrétienne, mise en musique plusieurs fois par Bach, tandis que le chiffre 6 représente une création incomplète et inacceptable. Cela peut expliquer pourquoi dans les Suites pour violoncelle, et dans bien d'autres, Bach a inséré le Prélude (et l'a composé plus tard) comme septième mouvement, couronnant les six danses, à l'instar de Marin Marais (moins précis quant au nombre de danses). En plus pour compléter les Suites Françaises, on peut ajouter les Préludes ou Préludes et Fugue de secours, y compris ceux du Clavier bien tempéré. Comme mentionné précédemment, le Prélude n'était pas seulement une composition qui préparait une atmosphère et un style particuliers pour la période ludique des danses, mais aussi une forme de divertissement plus virtuose et imaginative à écouter. En tout cas, j'ai proposé la « septième suite cachée » pour violoncelle et celle pour violon dans cette logique numérologique d'achèvement symbolique et la nécessité d'éviter les six 6 suites de six pièces. En ce qui concerne les quatre ensembles de Suites pour clavecin, je pense qu'il n'est pas nécessaire de chercher d'autres caractéristiques complexes dans certaines pièces pour fabriquer la septième Suite car il existe déjà de nombreuses suites sporadiques en dehors des groupements établis.

2.7   *Extension de l'analyse à d'autres chefs-d'œuvre*

De la liste des Suites et des observations ci-dessus, de nombreux autres canons multiples sont encore cachés et découvrables par les lecteurs sceptiques, tant dans les Partitas et Sonates que dans les Suites pour clavecin, ou pour luth : voir c'est croire. Je les ai gardés pour une improbable période de retraite !

Pour comprendre si les canons multiples cachés étaient une constante systématique chez J.S. Bach, ne me limitant pas aux Suites, je me suis lancé dans l'analyse de quelques Concertos. J'ai trouvé ce qui suit :

1) dans le Concerto pour violon BWV 1041, la partie de violon solo cache un canon à trois voix, c'est-à-dire qu'elle peut être jouée par trois solistes !

2) dans le Concerto pour deux violons BWV 1043 les deux parties solos cachent des canons à quatre voix, c'est-à-dire que la pièce peut être jouée à huit solistes !

3) Dans le Concerto pour hautbois et violon BWV 1060R chacune des deux voix solistes cache un canon à quatre voix, c'est-à-dire qu'il peut être joué avec 8 solistes, 4 violons et 4 hautbois ! De plus, même les quatre cordes de l'orchestre du

premier mouvement pourraient fonctionner en canon à quatre voix, de sorte que quatre orchestres peuvent jouer le morceau en même temps...

4) dans l'Allegro du 5ème Brandebourgeois, les parties de flûte seule et de violon seul sont compatibles avec des canons à quatre voix, c'est-à-dire que la pièce peut être jouée avec 4 violons et 4 flûtes seules.

5) Je n'ai pas pu trouver de canons cachés fonctionnels dans les autres mouvements du 5ème Brandeburgeois, cela signifie que :

    a) J.S. Bach n'a peut-être utilisé les canons cachés que s'il en avait le temps ou l'envie, ou il a délégué à sa femme ou à ses enfants la tâche d'achever les pièces de l'« usine Bach », sans mentionner les canons cachés.

    b) en tout cas la composition contrapuntique par elle-même n'implique pas la possibilité de trouver de canons multiples cachés !

Toutes les partitions issues de cette recherche sont disponibles gratuitement sur les sites IMSLP (voir les rubriques "arrangements" et "autres") et AIMAmusic (https://aimamusic.it/nuova-musica/).

2.8 *Objections contrapuntiques*

Certains musiciens m'ont dit que trouver des canons dans une composition contrapuntique allait de soi : cette observation est valable (et pas toujours) pour des canons à deux voix, ou pour des mélodies simples avec un mouvement oscillant, répété en cycles réguliers, comme celui exemplifié par Bach dans le canon BWV 1072, mais cela devient totalement faux lorsqu'il s'agit de canons à trois voix et de mélodies complexes comme celles des Suites : il suffit que certaines mesures changent d'une manière incompatible avec celle des mesures précédentes, comme les mesures problématiques de la deuxième Suite pour violoncelle, ou celles des autres mouvements du 5ème Brandebourgeois, tout en conservant un style contrapuntique. Si vous n'êtes pas convaincus, essayez de composer un canon à trois voix et vous comprendrez, ou bien cherchez des doubles canons cachés chez d'autres auteurs de pièces contrapuntiques !

Le chapitre suivant fournit des éclaircissements supplémentaires sur la complexité des canons multiples de Bach, et ce ne sont pas les plus connus, basés sur le guide-testament BWV 1087.

3   La difficulté de composer des canons multiples

3.1   Qu'est-ce qu'un canon ?

Le canon, au sens musical, est une manière intéressante d'accompagner une mélodie en utilisant la même mélodie retardée dans le temps comme seconde voix. D'un point de vue symbolique, le canon représente les différentes générations qui coexistent à différents moments de leur existence, naissent et meurent à des moments échelonnés dans le temps, les unes après les autres. Le canon est souvent utilisé dans des formes cycliques infinies, relançant la mélodie dès qu'elle se termine et donnant forme sonore au "panta rei" des anciens Grecs, l'histoire se répétant indéfiniment, ou à la métempsycose hindoue.

Du point de vue pratique de la composition, chaque élément de la mélodie composée pour fonctionner comme un canon, doit pouvoir se chevaucher aussi bien avec l'élément suivant qu'avec le précédent. La longueur de « l'élément » peut souvent correspondre au délai entre les entrées.

Dans les chansons populaires, on trouve souvent une forme simplifiée du canon, dans laquelle les éléments de la mélodie se répètent ou s'alternent, identiques à eux-mêmes, de sorte que seuls deux éléments compatibles entre eux suffisent. La représentation graphique de ces **"canons triviaux"** peut se faire en utilisant une couleur pour chaque élément de la mélodie, en les dessinant sur la ligne du temps qui s'écoule :

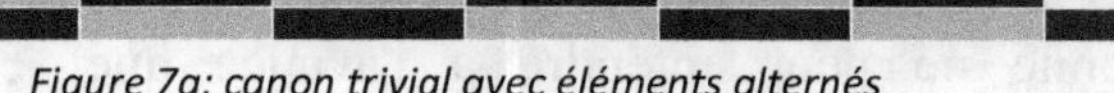

Figure 7a: canon trivial avec éléments alternés

On peut observer que ces canons triviaux fonctionnent également en ajoutant d'autres voix, mais dans le cas des éléments alternés de la figure 7a, la troisième voix est identique à la première, tandis que dans le cas des éléments répétés de la figure 7b, la cinquième voix est identique à la première.

Figure 7b: canon trivial avec éléments répétés

Dans les deux cas, les éléments qui se chevauchent sont toujours les mêmes et ce type de musique est écœurante et utilisé pour les chansons pour enfants, qui aiment les activités répétées de manière obsessionnelle. Néanmoins, l'effet de superposition d'une mélodie échelonnée sur elle-même crée une nouvelle sensation, un plaisir sui generis et un nouvel élément d'ensemble : c'est l'élément de base de la *métamusique* [11].

On peut en outre trouver des « **canons évolutifs** », dans lesquels les éléments qui se succèdent changent continuellement, ne se répètent jamais. Dans cette forme chaque élément doit être agréablement compatible simultanément avec l'élément suivant et avec le précédent, qui ne sont pas identiques comme dans le canon trivial. La représentation graphique devient la suivante :

Figure 8: canon évolutif simple avec éléments toujours différents

Ce canon est plus intéressant et "difficile" à composer par rapport aux précédents et évite les répétitions mièvres.

3.2   Canons multiples

À partir de la troisième voix ("double canon" ou "contre-canon"), la complexité augmente considérablement et presque personne ne peut entendre à l'avance quel effet aura la superposition et si une mélodie pourra satisfaire aux exigences du canon à trois voix : chacun des éléments de la mélodie doit en effet être compatible avec les deux éléments précédents et avec les deux éléments suivants :

Figure 9: double canon évolutif (à 3 voix)

Plus le nombre de voix à superposer dans un canon évolutif augmente, plus la complexité de composition de chaque élément et celle de l'écoute augmentent : pour n voix chaque élément doit être compatible avec $2 \times (n-1)$ éléments. Par exemple, pour 5 voix chaque élément doit être compatible avec 8 éléments (4 avant et 4 après), comme indiqué dans le schéma ci-dessous :

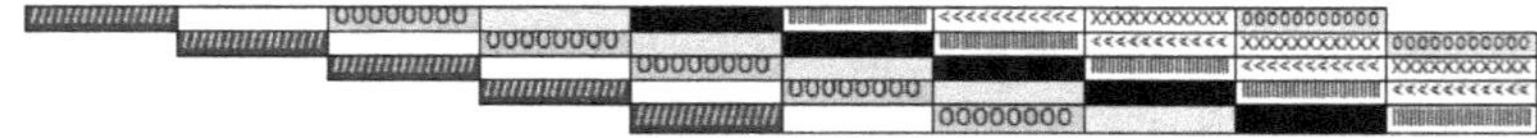

Figure 10: canon évolutif à 5 voix

Maintenant vous comprenez un peu mieux pourquoi j'ai eu du mal avec les mesures manquantes du Prélude de la deuxième Suite et vous comprenez aussi que créer le canon à huit voix de la Figure 1 n'est pas très simple, même avec l'aide d'un ordinateur, encore moins s'il doit aussi être agréable : pensez maintenant aux canons à sept voix des Suites et au canon à dix voix de la Gigue de la dernière Suite pour violoncelle. La présence de canons multiples cachés, immanents, explique pleinement la forme alambiquée particulière et le style étrange des mélodies de Bach, que l'on peut observer en les comparant à celles d'autres auteurs et qui m'ont toujours intrigué bien avant de faire cette découverte.

3.3 *Contexte canonique à l'époque de Bach*

Pour une information plus complète, je vous invite à vous référer aux travaux de Denis Collins [1] et [4]. Permettez-moi de faire quelques observations. Vu le contexte modeste de J.S. Bach pendant les années passées à Ohrdruf, hébergé par son frère ainé, l'organiste Johann Christoph, avec peu de partitions (coûteuses) à copier, peut-être en cachette, ou à mémoriser, il semble peu probable que J.S.B. ait pu découvrir les Ricercari, canons et sonates pour 2 violoncelles de Domenico Gabrielli (1689), qui étaient des canons évolutifs sous une forme simplifiée, alternant des tronçons de mélodie à une voix avec des tronçons d'accompagnement lorsque la mélodie passe à la deuxième voix. Au contraire il semble certain que dans le milieu culturel germanique Bach connut le célèbre Canon et Gigue en ré majeur, (1680, P.37) de Johann Pachelbel, qui avait été le professeur de son frère : cette pièce a une ligne de basso ostinato et trois voix sous la forme d'un canon évolutif simplifié, avec une alternance de phrases et d'accompagnements ; les éléments sont longs, mais restent dans la même tonalité et l'harmonie est somme toute médiocre. Malgré, ou peut-être grâce à cette simplicité, le Canon de Pachelbel reste un succès mondial et fut sans aucun doute une découverte et une référence pour le jeune Bach.

3.4 *Les canons évolutifs et modulants de Bach*

Ceci étant dit, les deux pièces citées ci-dessus restent dans la même tonalité du début à la fin. Au contraire, les canons évolutifs de Bach exigent un niveau de compatibilité plus élevé entre les éléments adjacents, car ils peuvent être dans des tonalités différentes (mélodie modulante). Les canons évolutifs à trois voix sont déjà difficiles à composer dans la même tonalité, mais ils demandent le talent d'un génie pour moduler et conserver de belles mélodies. Bach a probablement appris à changer de tonalité facilement lors de son aventure à Lübeck, avec un voyage à pied de 400 km pour espionner le célèbre organiste-improvisateur Dietrich Buxtehude avec son style « phantasticus » et ses Préludes et Fugues.

Certes les canons-crabe, ou ceux réfléchis, ou ceux « per augmentationem ou diminutionem » du BWV 1087 sont encore plus complexes d'un point de vue théorique, en revanche ils sont moins audibles et peu agréables sans support visuel. En tout cas, l'étude de ce petit livre porte sur des canons audibles, modulants, multiples, cachés.

4   Commentaires sur les « Guides aux canons»

4.1   Les petits guides des canons

Dans les partitions indiquées dans les références vous trouverez tous les débuts des différentes pièces avec les différents retards entre les entrées du canon pour les Suites françaises "complétées" et pour les anglaises et aussi pour les différents Concertos que j'ai explorés. Le fait de n'indiquer que le début des morceaux, en plus d'économiser du papier, permet aux musiciens de continuer à utiliser leur édition habituelle et de n'appliquer que le délai lorsqu'ils jouent avec d'autres musiciens. Les Suites pour violoncelle, en revanche, sont rapportées entièrement car j'ai eu la mauvaise idée de les "corriger", comme je l'expliquais précédemment, ce que je ne referais pas, car la découverte des canons cachés est le principal intérêt de cet ouvrage et parce que les variantes proposées dans les mélodies bien que plus compatibles avec les canons multiples sont toujours moins belles que l'original, même dans les cas où certaines pièces manquaient (fin de la sixième Suite), ou étaient visiblement rafistolées (deuxième Suite pour violoncelle) et un travail de « restauration conservatrice » serait nécessaire, pour les musicologues patients. Aussi certaines pièces particulières des Suites pour violon, la Suite « complétée » pour flûte, et les arrangements pour trio à cordes (violon-alto-violoncelle), ou pour fanfare d'instruments à vent, sont rapportés avec des partitions complètes pour permettre une exécution plus aisée. Ils sont tous sur les sites IMSLP et AIMAmusic.

4.2   Les incroyables rythmes syncopés cachés

La complexité rythmique que l'on peut observer dans certaines pièces est le côté le plus surprenant et le plus controversé de ces canons cachés à trois voix. Du point de vue des détracteurs potentiels, cela pourrait être décrit comme une astuce triviale pour échapper aux accords dissonants, car les notes sont plus délicatement échelonnées dans le temps et cela peut sembler un dispositif inapproprié pour l'époque de Bach. Mais après avoir cherché des solutions pendant un certain temps, je peux vous assurer que cette "astuce" ne fonctionne pas pour toutes les pièces, lorsqu'aucun canon décent n'est trouvé, cela crée simplement de la confusion. On retrouve d'ailleurs la même complexité rythmique des contretemps dans les archétypes pédagogiques proposés par Bach dans le guide BWV 1072. La conséquence en est que ce rythme immanent, typique des rhapsodies romantiques et des Ragtimes du XXe siècle, a été découvert par Bach et il ne l'a sans doute pas révélé car c'était trop moderne pour l'époque et certainement trop déstabilisant pour les danses de cour, très éloignées des bals modernes.

4.3   L'ambiance d'église lors de l'écoute des canons multiples

À l'exception des pièces mentionnées précédemment aux effets rythmiques étonnants, les autres pièces canoniques analysées créent une atmosphère et un son de musique d'église, plein d'échos et de résonances. Lors d'une écoute prolongée, à cause de l'attention et de la concentration que leur complexité exige, ils nous fatiguent. Cela explique aussi pourquoi Bach n'a pas proposé les versions explicites à plusieurs canons de ces pièces, à jouer avec plusieurs instruments, malgré le gain plus élevé qui aurait pu été obtenu (les partitions étaient payées en fonction de leur longueur et de leur nombre de notes !) : elles auraient été bien moins appréciées que les versions pour un seul instrument. Pourquoi alors se donner tant de mal pour composer des canons multiples et les garder cachés ? La deuxième partie du livre tente de répondre à cette question.

2ème Partie COMPRENDRE c'est VIVRE

5 La nécessité est la mère de toute vertu

Il est temps maintenant d'essayer de comprendre pourquoi J.S. Bach a composé ses mélodies d'une manière si particulière, et

Fig. 11 Johann Sebastian Bach (agé de 61 ans) portrait de Elias Gottlob Haussmann, seconde version du brouillon de 1746. Bach présente son canon à six voix BWV 1076.
http://www.jsbach.net/bass/elements/bach-hausmann.jpg , https://commons.wikimedia.org/w/index.php?curid=1270015

pourquoi il en était si fier qu'il a inclus plusieurs canons dans son testament-portrait comme l'achèvement de l'œuvre de toute une vie.

Même son Monogramme (sceau) a une couronne au centre : il avait conscience d'être (et sera toujours) le Roi des canons. Une observation plus précise du sceau révèle des séries de trois lignes parallèles, qui peuvent rappeler les canons à trois voix, en miroir, pour peut-être indiquer des triples canons inverses, encore à découvrir quelque part ...

Fig.12 Sceau de Bach, au centre, utilisé à l'époque de Leipzig. Il contient ses initiales J S B réfléchies et assemblées. Sur les cotés on voit le détail.

https://commons.wikimedia.org/wiki/File:Bach_Seal.svg#filelinks

5.1 La vie extraordinaire de J.S. Bach

On ne peut pas être fier d'un talent acquis à la naissance, mais si on l'a développé au prix d'exercices et d'une vie difficile, alors on peut vraiment l'être.

Johann Sebastian était le dernier de sept enfants, protégé et certainement choyé par ses parents, frères et sœurs et aussi éduqué musicalement par d'autres oncles musiciens. Il jouait et s'amusait sur de nombreux instruments différents, du violon au clavecin et a grandi insouciant dans un petit village du Saint Romain Empire d'Occident. Il n'avait que neuf ans lorsque sa mère est décédée, son père n'a pu survivre que quelques mois et la famille s'est effondrée. Le paradis de l'enfance était perdu à jamais. Son frère aîné avait heureusement déjà un travail d'organiste à l'église Saint-Michel d'Ohrdruf et l'hébergea avec un autre frère cadet. L'école n'était hélas pas un refuge pour lui (c.f. [13]). On peut imaginer que dans cette nouvelle vie J.S. trouva refuge à l'église, où il apprit à jouer de l'orgue auprès de son frère, pour le plaisir, mais devint ainsi lui-même musicien. Il apprenait sûrement les morceaux par cœur et quand il le pouvait il copiait toutes les précieuses partitions en circulation, au risque d'être puni pour avoir gaspillé le dispendieux papier, pour découvrir la musique des compositeurs du sud de l'Allemagne, les jouer et comprendre comment ils composaient. Il était intelligent et brillant, à tel point qu'il fut sélectionné pour une bourse à la célèbre école Saint-Michel de Lüneburg. L'important pour nous est qu'il passa certainement beaucoup de temps à jouer des orgues d'église, surmontant ainsi toutes les tendances autistiques causées par le traumatisme d'être orphelin, car il devint un champion d'improvisation.

5.2 L'acoustique architecturale comme contexte déclencheur

Dans le monde de J.S. Bach, la musique était jouée dans les temples luthériens, nus et austères, ou dans les salles vides aux murs de pierre des palais, enrichies tout au plus de quelques tapisseries. D'un point de vue acoustique, ces deux types d'espaces étaient caractérisés par un long temps de réverbération et par quelques échos dominants. Dans les églises dites Hallenkirchen, avec une même hauteur sous plafond dans la nef et dans les bas-côtés, les deux échos principaux correspondaient l'un à la longueur de la nef et l'autre à la hauteur constante de l'église. Il en résultait surement un certain chaos acoustique et une écoute très difficile de la musique et des discours, surtout à des distances supérieures à deux ou trois mètres des musiciens, ou des orateurs. Les espaces acoustiquement meilleurs auraient pu être les cloîtres, les cours et les places publiques, mais le climat allemand limitait leur utilisation à la saison chaude, ou aux instruments à vent, moins sensibles aux variations de température et d'humidité que les instruments utilisant le boyau pour leurs cordes. L'autre alternative acoustiquement valable étaient les tavernes bondées, mais c'étaient des endroits pour les ménestrels et les musiciens qu'aucun compositeur n'aurait pris en considération (parce qu'il n'aurait pas partagé les gages des exécutants). Dans les églises catholiques baroques, grâce à la variété des formes, chapelles, niches, statues, colonnes et innombrables ornements en stuc, panneaux de bois, qui faisaient office de diffuseurs naturels, la présence des échos était atténuée et un génie comme Bach n'aurait pas eu le besoin et l'occasion de résoudre ce problème. De même à notre époque avec des panneaux d'insonorisation. Le fait est que pour le jeune Bach qui passait son temps sur les orgues de l'église d'Ohrdruf (une Hallenkirche), le problème acoustique majeur était d'obtenir une musique claire et tranchante, luttant contre les résonances et grondements omniprésents, les superpositions disharmoniques, le désordre sonore : cette confusion était d'autant plus inacceptable qu'elle était incompatible avec la notion d'ordre et d'harmonie, fondamentale à sa religion et à la philosophie leibnizienne qui avait imprégné sa formation.

5.3 *La solution géniale de Bach*

Après avoir trouvé tant de canons à trois voix, je suis arrivé à la **thèse** que la solution géniale que le jeune Bach développa pour faire face au problème acoustique de la confusion des échos et de la réverbération dans les salles où il jouait fut *d'adapter la musique, de manière* à *obtenir une superposition harmonieuse* *avec les échos*, sorte de synergie temporelle avec le son émis auparavant par son instrument.

Pour arriver à cette découverte **deux dons exceptionnels** lui ont été nécessaires. Le premier, un grand talent pour adapter son interprétation aux événements sonores extérieurs, aussi appelé « *improvisation entraînée* » : le désir intense de nouveauté et la capacité d'improviser librement, lui a été *donné en cadeau par l'ennui*, une fois explorées, exploitées et épuisées les partitions de son frère. Le second don, un *développement extraordinaire de l'ouïe*, avec une attention maniacale/autistique aux échos et à l'effet global de la musique dans le milieu environnant et pas seulement aux notes qu'émet l'instrument, une capacité d'écoute omnisciente, incubée dans l'église de Ohrdruf, fut *un don de la solitude et du silence*.

La célèbre capacité d'improvisation de J.S. Bach dérive de sa riche *imagination mélodique* ajoutée à son *contrôle* auditif extrême. Il était capable en effet d'imaginer le recouvrement de chaque élément joué avec les éléments joués auparavant, renvoyés par les murs, et avec les éléments dans sa tête qu'il allait jouer. Cette modalité d'exécution coïncide avec l'essence du canon et les deux échos des Hallenkirchen imposent des canons à trois voix.

Espace-temps. En analysant les canons cachés dans les différentes Suites de Bach (celles françaises et anglaises, ou celles pour violoncelle, violon ou flûte) on s'aperçoit que le délai entre les voix varie généralement d'un quart de seconde à environ une demi-seconde, cela correspond à une longueur de la nef entre quarante et quatre-vingts mètres : très vraisemblable. Les premières pièces pour orgue que Bach a écrites, par exemple la Fugue en ut BWV Anh.107, ou la Fantaisie en ut majeur BWV 570 cachent également des canons. Cela soutient assez bien ma théorie suivante : *je suppose que la formation auditive et les premières expériences d'improvisation de Bach ont eu lieu à Ohrdruf, tandis que son élaboration consciente et son* *raffinement technique ont eu lieu dans les années d'études suivantes* à Lüneburg et dans les premières années de travail. Je n'ai pas encore eu le plaisir d'analyser les compositions de Dietrich Buxtehude, que Bach était allé espionner à Lübeck, et qui utilisait abondamment la structure de la fugue, mais je ne pense pas pouvoir y trouver des canons multiples cachés : c'est certainement l'invention de Bach, basée sur son expérience de vie. Même la technique exécutive basée sur des canons immanents (cachés) explique pleinement le succès de J.S. Bach dans les concours d'improvisation : il adaptait le son émis avec celui qui retournait dans l'espace, en obtenant des harmonies riches, des sons nets et clairs. C'est devenu son *ingrédient secret* et il a peut-être essayé de l'enseigner et de le transmettre à sa femme et à ses enfants comme on peut le voir dans les guides BWV 1072-86 et 1087, mais ils ont emporté ce secret dans la tombe.

J'ai validé cette hypothèse de l'objectif acoustique d'obtenir une écoute claire et nette en champs diffus avec écho réalisé par Bach à l'aide des canons lors de l'écoute d'un concert d'orgue dans une grande église avec une mauvaise acoustique : seules les pièces de Bach ressortaient nettement du bruit de fond confus, les morceaux d'autres auteurs restaient noyés dans les grondements.

En support supplémentaire à ma thèse, je dois mentionner que Bach a montré un grand intérêt pour le **phénomène des échos** : plusieurs de ses compositions s'appellent Echo (dans BVW 821, 831, 1002). A noter que l'intérêt pour les échos et leur utilisation dans les morceaux de musique se manifeste déjà dès la Renaissance, avec H. Vecchi, A. Banchieri, G. Gabrieli..., ou à des époques plus proches de Bach, avec I. Posch, G. Sronx (Echo en fa majeur 1617), S. Scheidt (Echo ad manual duplex 1624), C. de Tallard (Air in Echo, Suite pour Lute) et plus tard dans A. Lotti (Sonate a 4 : Echo - Adagio-Presto 1717), A. Vivaldi (RV552, Concerto pour violon principal avec autre violon en écho 1740) et chez des dizaines de compositeurs plus récents dans l'histoire de la musique, mais vous pouvez comprendre maintenant que Bach est le maître incontesté de tous.

A plusieurs reprises, J.S. Bach a tenté de faire ajouter des clochettes sur les orgues de Mühlhausen, alors qu'il était chargé d'en suivre la construction et l'accord. Cette idée peut sembler saugrenue : les orgues comportent déjà plusieurs claviers et jeux, ils regorgent de timbres et de sonorités différents. Cette idée lui est venue sur les orgues d'Arnstadt qui avaient le Cymbelstern (carrousel de cloches), mais contrairement au Cymbelstern, qui tournait et déplaçait automatiquement les cloches avec l'air sortant des tuyaux, de manière aléatoire et chaotique, Bach voulait que le les cloches fussent commandées par un clavier, frappé précisément par des marteaux, comme les cordes d'un clavecin. Au-delà de son goût de l'ordre et de la précision, mon interprétation d'acousticien est qu'il avait besoin d'un son très différent de celui de l'orgue, avec une attaque très précise dans le temps, pour se repérer par rapport aux échos présents dans l'église et gérer le son des improvisations avec des canons cachés.

Un petit **excès de scrupules** : l'objection scientifique à ma thèse pourrait être que les différents échos ne reviennent généralement pas à intervalles de temps réguliers (c'est-à-dire que les deux échos cités n'ont pas le même retard !), surtout si la taille de la pièce, ou la distance de la source sonore (musicien) aux murs ne sont pas les bonnes. Je ne peux que supposer et conclure que dans l'église d'Ohrdruf (qui a été détruite par un incendie et me laisse libre de rêver) la position des orgues et les dimensions étaient telles qu'elles garantissaient la situation susmentionnée : par exemple si les orgues étaient situés à l'extrémité de la nef centrale et si celle-ci était deux fois plus grande que la hauteur de l'église (comme par hasard identique à sa largeur), alors les échos auraient eu la distribution régulière requise dans le temps. Permettez-moi une dernière précision : les pièces que j'ai longuement analysées (les Suites) ne sont pas destinées à la musique d'orgues/d'église, mais à celle de chambre, ou salle de palais, de la *période de Weimar* (1708-1717) et de *Köthen*, donc j'imagine que même dans les salles du palais ducal, Bach a rencontré des problèmes similaires à ceux de l'église d'Ohrdruf. L'œuvre pour orgue de Bach doit être analysée plus en détail au regard des canons cachés pour confirmer pleinement ma thèse sur l'origine physique du « phénomène Bach » dans l'église d'Ohrdruf. Une genèse à l'époque de Weimar serait plus facile à soutenir, car en musique de chambre on peut choisir la position de l'instrumentiste de manière stratégique d'un point de vue acoustique, alors que pour les orgues ce n'est pas possible.

6 Mémoire acoustique et effet psychoacoustique

6.1 *La mémoire acoustique*

Selon les concepts de base de la psychoacoustique, la mémoire acoustique des personnes normales est très courte, notamment pour les bruits qui ne donnent pas d'information: par exemple, si vous voulez comparer les bruits de deux configurations d'un véhicule, vous devez effectuer les tests en succession très rapprochée, ou vous devez enregistrer et comparer les deux sons avec une écoute au casque. Pour d'autres sons, liés à la survie humaine, grâce à l'évolution physiologique, l'ouïe est beaucoup plus sensible et peut capter de petites variations dans le bruit environnant habituel, du bruit d'un moustique, au craquement d'une feuille sèche, au dysfonctionnement d'une machine. En général, lorsqu'une information ou une émotion est associée à l'écoute, le cerveau est plus précis et attentif. En parlant d'oreilles entraînées, les musiciens n'ont aucun problème à distinguer des intervalles d'un 24ème octave (quart de ton), ou à se souvenir d'une mélodie, ou d'un morceau de musique complexe en termes de fréquences (harmonies) et d'événements temporels (rythmes) et certains sont capables de se souvenir de la valeur exacte des fréquences (on parle d'« oreille absolue »), ou pour évaluer si l'amplitude du son a augmenté, ou diminué avec le temps. Cela leur donne la possibilité d'ajuster la dynamique de jeu en amplitude et en vitesse. Ils peuvent enregistrer dans leur tête des heures entières de musique. La même chose arrive aux acteurs avec des textes de poésie ou de théâtre et à de nombreux religieux avec des livres de textes sacrés mémorisés.

D'autre part, on peut observer que même des personnes non formées peuvent se souvenir de mélodies, ou de poèmes courts, ou de phrases simplement entendues et que *l'interprétation du son entendu prend du temps* : par exemple pour le langage, lorsque plusieurs personnes parlent en même temps et que c'est important de suivre tous les discours. En d'autres termes, on peut dire que le son utile est « maintenu en vie » dans le cerveau pendant un certain temps, comme s'il réverbérait dans une chambre vide, dans une sorte de *mémoire tampon interprétative.* En revenant au pays de Bach, on peut constater (et Charlie Chaplin l'a fait avec brio dans « Le grand dictateur » !) que la structure grammaticale des phrases allemandes, qui suspend la détermination du sens jusqu'au verbe final, nécessite d'une mémoire interprétative plus longue. Ce temps de traitement, systématique et inconscient dans notre cerveau, existe aussi bien pour la parole que pour la musique : cela signifie que pendant que nous entendons un son, *le son précédent est présent dans notre mémoire, y coexiste et ils se superposent.*

6.2   La deuxième intuition de Bach

Je pense que Bach a observé et compris cette dynamique mentale à l'époque d'Ohrdruf (où Ohr signifie oreille et Ruf signifie appel, et qui était donc le lieu idéal pour une vocation auditive de Bach !). Je fais l'hypothèse qu'il a fait remonter à un état conscient et contrôlé un phénomène qui pour d'autres est inconscient et qu'il s'en est servi pour gagner ses concours d'improvisation et obtenir des effets harmoniques et des sensations extraordinaires dans le cerveau des auditeurs, où la musique s'accompagne et s'enrichit grâce au contenu précédent de la mémoire.

Puisque la mémoire interprétative acoustique ne dépend pas de la présence physique d'un écho dans le lieu d'écoute, l'efficacité de l'approche de Bach concerne l'expérience auditive commune. Cette deuxième partie de ma thèse pourrait donc être considérée comme une négation de la première partie : pas de problèmes physiques d'écho à résoudre, pas d'acoustique des salles, seulement un fonctionnement psychoacoustique du cerveau et l'intuition géniale de Bach.

Je préfère penser que les deux explications coexistent, car j'aime les deux et je ne suis pas intellectuellement monogame. J'ai personnellement expérimenté l'explication physique (l'acoustique des salles) et la seconde (la psychoacoustique) est en théorie plus difficile à démontrer (je n'ai pas encore fait d'électroencéphalogramme sur les musicologues !), mais vous pouvez l'expérimenter vous-même en vous concentrant sur ce que vous entendez et sur ce qui résonne dans votre mémoire à l'écoute des pièces de Bach.

En tout cas, même en ne considérant que l'explication psychique, l'indication de maintenir un tempo stable lors de l'exécution de ces pièces de Bach reste valable.

6.3   La stratégie derrière les canons cachés

Lorsque j'ai découvert les premiers canons à trois ou sept voix dans les Suites (pour violoncelle, violon ou flûte), j'ai pensé que c'était une stratégie ingénieuse de Bach pour obtenir l'effet d'un concert polyphonique avec un seul instrument mélodique, très utile et bon marché pour les voyages de la cour du prince Léopold de Köthen. C'était probablement un "effet secondaire", je ne savais pas encore que Bach avait placé plusieurs canons cachés dans ses premières œuvres de Weimar : les Suites anglaise et française pour clavecin ! A cela s'ajoute qu'il continuera à composer ainsi plus tard aussi, pour de plus grands ensembles : plusieurs concertos pour orchestre et solistes contiennent de canons multiples cachés. Alors l'hypothèse des "kits de voyage" s'est complètement effondrée et il a fallu trouver une autre explication : la thèse précédemment exposée sur l'effet de clarté et de netteté sonore obtenu dans des environnements hostiles (acoustique des salles) et l'enrichissement des sensations d'écoute (psychoacoustique).

6.4 *Pourquoi resté caché aussi longtemps ?*

Les Suites pour instruments solistes sont des pièces de Bach où les canons cachés se découvrent plus facilement; cela m'est donc arrivé en tant que violoncelliste, mais aussi grâce à la passion pour l'analyse de textes et des contextes historico-philosophiques que m'a transmise mon oncle, à l'intérêt pour les religions et la psychologie que mon père m'a laissé, à la compréhension scientifique des phénomènes acoustiques qu'un doctorat m'a donnée, à une familiarité d'ingénieur avec les ordinateurs, à une méthode de composition contrapuntique métamusicale [11] et à une certaine insistance autistique. C'est toujours l'aboutissement, le résultat qui attire à lui tous les éléments nécessaires, de manière imprévisible, incohérente et improbable. Le prince Léopold en bon calviniste aurait parlé de prédestination, d'univers nécessaire.

Pourquoi personne n'a remarqué ces canons multiples cachés dans les mélodies de Bach depuis trois siècles ? Je vais essayer de donner quelques explications possibles : les Suites de danse étaient une forme tombée en désuétude au dix-huitième siècle, les danses de cour, éphémères et mondaines, ont changé, celles proposées par Bach étaient inutilisables; puis la musique pour instruments solistes s'est déplacée des cours des nobles vers les salons bourgeois, plus petits, bien habillés de drapages et sans écho, de plus les pièces de Bach, symboles d'équilibre et d'harmonie, bien que virtuoses, n'avaient pas un goût assez romantique; enfin les partitions étaient trop chères pour les musiciens de rue.

Néanmoins, les suites de Bach ont été étudiées par de grands compositeurs tels que Mendelssohn, et la musique de Bach a influencé Haydn, Mozart, Beethoven et de nombreux compositeurs après eux, mais personne n'a remarqué les canons raffinés, ni le portrait du testament. La fugue semblait plus complexe et exigeante que les canons pour un compositeur et pour les musicologues. Cet oubli implique également qu'aucun des membres de la famille de Bach n'a jamais révélé l'ingrédient secret de la "boite", malgré l'état de pauvreté d'Anna Magdalena : ils ont probablement juré de ne rien dire, ou ils ne l'ont jamais su. On devrait étudier leurs pièces...

Même à notre époque romantique tardive, des solistes comme Casals, Glenn Gould, qui ont passé leur vie avec les Suites, ont exploité leur beauté pour exprimer leur talent, sans s'apercevoir des trésors qu'elles cachaient. Il faut avouer qu'il est vraiment difficile d'ignorer l'attrait et le plaisir que suscite leur interprétation, les mélodies changent constamment de style et d'ambiance et on ne peut pas imaginer qu'elles cachent des canons.

6.5 Dernière révision des Suites

Après avoir formulé l'explication physique du jeu avec les échos, j'ai remis en question ma première analyse des Suites pour violoncelle : les délais des voix dans le temps étaient trop longs par rapport aux Suites que j'ai analysées plus tard et par rapport aux dimensions des salles. J'ai ainsi trouvé des solutions avec des délais plus courts qui n'imposent aucun changement dans les Préludes de la deuxième Suite et de la première Suite. Toutes les élucubrations sur les « trous » laissés dans les partitions et complétés par Anna Magdalena, des paragraphes 2.5 et 2.6, bien que séduisantes et drôles, avec ces nouvelles solutions ne sont plus nécessaires. Le début de la 2ème Suite devient :

Tout ce travail serait donc né d'une écoute erronée du Prélude de

la deuxième Suite, faite selon l'habitude de chanter des canons avec des retards d'environ une mesure : une erreur fructueuse, sans laquelle les vrais canons n'auraient pas revu le jour. J'ai réanalysé diverses pièces et mis les nouvelles versions des partitions sur les sites IMSLP et AIMAmusic.

Il convient également de noter que les courts délais entre les voix limitent les chevauchements entre différentes tonalités à des segments de musique plus courts et facilitent la composition de canons multiples évolutifs et modulants. L'écoute de courts délais n'a rien d'intuitif, elle est difficile et fait ressortir l'exceptionnalité des capacités auditives de J.S. Bach.

7 Conclusions

1. J'ai trouvé un trésor caché en suivant la carte vivante d'une partition, après des siècles d'attente patiente du compositeur : des précieux canons multiples évolutifs et modulants sont sertis comme des diamants et des émeraudes, immanents, invisibles, dans de nombreux chefs-d'œuvre de J.S. Bach.

2. En faisant cela, "en passant", j'ai mieux compris le sens de l'étrange voyage de ma vie.

3. Désormais, chacun peut entendre la complexité de la façon dont Bach a conçu son œuvre, redécouvrir ses chefs-d'œuvre sous une nouvelle lumière et explorer des capacités de sa propre ouïe.

4. Les musiciens peuvent jouer ensemble, ou seuls, assistés par quelques appareils audio, et trouver de nouvelles façons d'interpréter les classiques. Même le clonage de musiciens peut désormais avoir un sens !

5. Les musiciens peuvent être plus stratèges en choisissant l'endroit où ils jouent ou écoutent la musique de Bach dans une pièce acoustiquement hostile.

6. Les musicologues peuvent poursuivre leurs recherches sur les œuvres de Bach et découvrir d'autres mondes inattendus, ou perdre du temps à invalider ce travail s'ils le souhaitent.

7. Et si ce ne fut qu'un rêve, c'en fut un magnifique, digne d'être rêvé !

REFERENCES pour les PARTITIONS des CANONS CACHES

[A] Cello Suites https://imslp.org/wiki/File:PMLP4291-6CelloSuitesHiddenCanonsGuide.pdf

[B] Violin Suites best of
https://imslp.org/wiki/Special:ImagefromIndex/790271/vg25

[C] "completed" Flute Suite
https://imslp.org/wiki/Special:ImagefromIndex/788474/vg25

[D] "completed" French Suites
https://imslp.org/wiki/Special:ImagefromIndex/809911/vg25

[E] English Suites
https://imslp.org/wiki/Special:ImagefromIndex/809741/vg25

[F] Goldberg Variations Aria
https://imslp.org/wiki/Special:ImagefromIndex/809278/vg25

[G] Violin Concerto BWV 1041
https://imslp.org/wiki/Special:ImagefromIndex/821336/vg25

[H] 2 Violins Concerto BWV 1043
https://imslp.org/wiki/Special:ImagefromIndex/821337/vg25

[I] Oboe and Violin Concerto BWV 1060R
https://imslp.org/wiki/Special:ImagefromIndex/821335/vg25

[J] 5th Brandenburger BWV 1050 Allegro
https://imslp.org/wiki/Special:ImagefromIndex/822690/vg25

ECOUTES sur le WEB

https://www.youtube.com/channel/UCG4BI8Q1vR7SbMxCxDJ_yIA

https://metamusica.altervista.org/

Mini Bibliographie

[1.a] Denis Collins, *From Bull to Bach: In Search of Precedents for the "Complete" Version of the Canon by Augmentation and Contrary Motion in J. S. Bach's "Musical Offering"* Source: Bach, Vol. 38, No. 2 (2007), pp. 39-63 Published by: Riemenschneider Bach Institute.

[1.b] Dennis Collins and W. Andrew Schloss, *An Unusual Effect in the Canon Per Tonos from J. S. Bach's Musical Offering* Source: Music Perception: An Interdisciplinary Journal, Vol. 19, No. 2 (Winter 2001), pp. 141-153 Published by: University of California Press

[1.c] Denis Collins, *Bach and Approaches to Canonic Composition in Early Eighteenth-Century Theoretical and Chamber Music Sources*. Source: Bach, Vol. 30, No. 2 (1999), pp. 27-48 Published by: Riemenschneider Bach Institute

[2] Marcel Bitsch , *J.S. Bach, canons BWV 1087: analyse et commentaires* 1977, Durand, T. Presse

[3] Christoph Wolff, "Bach's Handexemplar of the Goldberg Variations: A New Source", Journal of the American Musicological Society XXIV/2 (Summer 1976), pp. 224-241.

[4] Denis Collins *Historical precedents for Bach's "evolutio" canon BWV1087/10* Source: Bach, vol. 24, No. 1 (Spring-Summer, 1993), pp. 5-14 Published by: Riemenschneider Bach Institute

[5] Alexander Maykapar, September 2, 2015 THE 13th CANON: Portrait of J.S. Bach In https://www.projectawe.org/blog?category=AWE https://www.projectawe.org/blog?category=maria+danova

[6a] Athanase Papadopoulos, *Mathématiques et musique chez J.S. Bach*, 2000, L'ouvert 100, papadopoulos@math.u-strasbg.fr

[6b] Martin Jarvis, *Written by Mrs Bach*, 2011, HarperCollins Publishers Australia. http://www.harpercollins.com.au/9780733328725/

[7] Tony Phillips, *Math and the Musical Offering*, https://www.ams.org/publicoutreach/feature-column/fcarc-canons

[8] J.S. Bach Crab Canon on a Moebius band
https://www.openculture.com/2009/09/how_a_bach_canon_works.html

[9a] Denis Collins, *Bach's Occasional Canon BWV 1073 and "Stacked" Canonic Procedure in the Eighteenth Century* Source: Bach, Vol. 33, No. 2 (2002), pp. 15-34 Published by: Riemenschneider Bach Institute

[9b] Albert Clement, *Johann Sebastian Bach and the praise of God, some thoughts on the canon triplex (BWV 1076),* In: Music and theology: essays in honor of Robin A. Leaver/ed. by Daniel Zager-Lanham, Md.[u.a.], 2007.- S. 147-168

[10] Dr. Timothy A. Smith, Northern Arizona University *Canons and Fugues of J.S. Bach*, Tutorial 2020-2021

[11] https://metamusica.altervista.org/spiegazioni/generalinfo.html

[12] Bob van Asperen, contrib. F. Huneau, M. Quagliozzi, *François Dieupart's Biography Revised and the Genesis and Dating of his Six Suittes de Clavessin, with Remarks on their Influence on J.S. Bach*. Amsterdam, 2021

[13] John Eliot Gardiner, *Bach: Music in the Castle of Heaven,* 2013

Informations sur l'auteur

Giovanni Pietro Orefice (Milano 1967-Gap-Grenoble-Lyon-Berlin-Paris-Torino-Milano/Desenzano/Modena), Doctorat d'Acoustique, Violoncelliste, Compositeur de Métamusique (cf [11]).

Hidden canons samples – Beispiele von verborgenen Kanons – Esempi di canoni nascosti – Exemples de canons cachés.